*f*P

Crashing
the Borders

*How Basketball
Won the World and
Lost Its Soul at Home*

Harvey Araton

FREE PRESS

NEW YORK   LONDON   TORONTO   SYDNEY

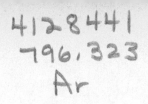

FREE PRESS
A Division of Simon & Schuster, Inc.
1230 Avenue of the Americas
New York, NY 10020

Free Press and colophon are trademarks of Simon & Schuster, Inc.

For information about special discounts for bulk purchases,
please contact Simon & Schuster Special Sales:
1-800-456-6798 or business@simonandschuster.com

Designed by Karolina Harris

Manufactured in the United States of America

10   9   8   7   6   5   4   3   2   1

Library of Congress Cataloging-in-Publication Data
Araton, Harvey.
    Crashing the borders : how basketball won the world and lost its soul at
home / Harvey Araton.
        p.   cm.
    Includes index.
    1. Basketball—United States—History—20th century.   2. Basketball—Social aspects—
United States.   I. Title.
GV883.A73 2005
796.323'64'0973—dc22   2005044906

ISBN-13: 978-0-7432-8069-3
ISBN-10:   0-7432-8069-5

The columns from which this book has been derived originally appeared in
The New York Times, and to the extent they are reprinted here, they are reprinted
with permission. Inquiries concerning permission to reprint any article or portion
thereof should be directed to The New York Times Company, News Services Division,
The Times Agency, Ninth Floor, 229 West 43rd Street, New York, New York 10036
or rights@nytimes.com.

Dedicated to the 1969–70 Knicks
and to the memory of Red Holzman and Dave DeBusschere.

Contents

Crashing
the Borders

Introduction

IF YOU HAVE EVER loved basketball, then you had to hate November 19, 2004. If you have relished the sounds and smells of the gymnasium—the sweet squeaking of sneaker soles, the rustling of nets, and, yes, even the chatter less euphemistically known as trash talk—then your senses came under assault by what you saw that night at The Palace of Auburn Hills in suburban Detroit. And the more times you watched the most frightening eruption of sustained violence ever in the American sports arena, the more you saw the replaying of a troubled young man named Ron Artest bolt from his reclining press-table position, across your television screen, and into everlasting infamy, the more angry you were and the more you hurt for the game that had brought so much joy into your life.

Since I was a young boy peering out my bedroom window at the netless rims of the basketball courts between Henderson Avenue buildings in the West Brighton Houses, a city project squeezed into a working-class neighborhood on Staten Island, I have loved the game. Loved it for its simplicity and accessibility, for the way it packed people of all shapes and sizes, races and ethnicities, into pressurized chambers of passion. Loved it for the freedom of individuality it promised within the framework of the collective. Loved it for the hours I could dribble my weathered ball down on the courts, even when they were empty in the dead of winter, and shoot and shoot until my fingers felt frostbit. Loved it to my five-foot-eight-inch playing limits, or for just being in the crowd when the kids with size and skills commanded the courts.

One of our blessed, Heyward Dotson, older than me by a few years, became a star at Stuyvesant High School and then all the way uptown at Columbia University. Occasionally, Dotson would bring Jim McMillian—a college teammate who went on to shine in the NBA—and other hotshot players from around the world's preeminent basketball city to New York's most isolated borough, to our unevenly paved oasis inside one of the Island's few pockets of relative poverty. We'd all gather round, watching in awe as these gods of the game communed at rim level.

One summer, when I was twelve or thirteen, my friends and I shuffled down to the courts for a clinic sponsored by the New York City Housing Authority. The main attraction was the impossibly tall and already famous UCLA underclassman, Lew Alcindor, along with a couple of Knicks backcourt reserves, Emmette Bryant and Fred Crawford. But it was another fellow, introduced as Mr. Bruce Spraggins from the New Jersey Americans of the brand-new American Basketball Association, who caught my attention, a six-five forward with a killer jump shot and no public profile.

When the Americans-cum-Nets prevailed after decades of misadventure to land in their first NBA Finals in June 2002, I wondered what had become of Spraggins and other franchise originals. I called Herb Turetzky, the only official scorer in the history of the franchise and a native of the same Brownsville neighborhood in Brooklyn that I had lived in until my family moved to Staten Island when I was ten. "Remember him?" Turetzky said. "Spraggins, Levern Tart, Tony Jackson—those are my guys." He put me in touch, and Spraggins, answering the telephone at his apartment on 107th Street and First Avenue in Manhattan, said, of course he recalled the clinic for the kids in the Staten Island projects. "When we had that shootout we'd always do after the instruction part, I don't think I missed more than one shot,"

Spraggins bragged, affirming my belief that lifelong basketball memories could be made anywhere there was a ball, a basket, and the ability to stretch the truth.

As a sportswriter and columnist for four New York City dailies, I've been lucky enough to accumulate a few decades' worth. I have covered my share of games in the dowdiest high-school gyms and in the swankiest of luxury-box palaces. Years of following the Knicks with a suitcase and a laptop have taught me to navigate my way around most American downtowns and even a few intersections of Los Angeles freeways. Beginning with the 1992 Barcelona Summer Olympics and the original (and one authentic) Dream Team, basketball has helped me travel the world, to places I never dreamed of as a child whose family never ventured beyond the Catskills. From Europe to Australia, all the way to Tbilisi in the Republic of Georgia, in what just a decade earlier was behind the Iron Curtain.

I visited with the family of a Denver Nuggets' 2002 first-round draft pick named Nikoloz Tskitishvili, for a project investigating the accelerating rate of foreign-born players coming from all corners of the globe. On the wall at the end of a foyer inside a one-bedroom flat, I noticed a poster of Michael Jordan soaring for one of his patented dunks. Further inspection revealed the familiar trappings of Madison Square Garden, and looking closer still, myself, hunched over the press table, eyes on the airborne Jordan.

Thrilled no end to find myself enshrined with Jordan in this remote city in the heart of the Caucasus, I summoned Tskitishvili's mother, and the small circle of relatives and friends present to meet *The New York Times* columnist who had traveled so far to talk about their Nikoloz, with the assistance of an interpreter. "Look, it's me," I said, finger to the poster, and suddenly there was pandemonium, hugs all around, my back and shoulders pounded, a bottle of wine opened, a toast offered in the finest of Georgian traditions. To me, "friend of Jordan."

While I didn't break it to them that I wasn't quite on the level of Ahmad Rashad, the Jordan sidekick moonlighting as a network cheerleader, I certainly was no stranger to the Jordan phenomenon, to the man who in many respects was the global face of American entertainment culture across the 1990s. From his first championship three-peat with the Bulls through the Salt Lake City followthrough on the title-winning jumper that capped his second, there was no escaping Jordan and, by extension, the NBA growth industry.

I couldn't imagine having wanted to, for what other game offered a sports journalist the kind of upfront access to the field of play I'd had back in the projects when Bruce Spraggins paid us a visit? Even when deadlines became impossibly demanding, as the games dragged later into the East Coast night, you could always count on a window opening during the course of the game, the kind of dramatic scene, audio included, unavailable in the distant baseball and pro football press boxes.

Several years ago, Pat Williams—one of pro basketball's more eclectic personalities, a personnel maven in Philadelphia and Orlando who doubled as a motivational speaker and quasi comic—called to say he was doing a book on Jordan and asked if I had a favorite story that best characterized the man. "That's easy," I told Williams, and proceeded to write him a few paragraphs about a 1992 playoff game, Chicago at New York, a brutal seven-game series in which the game plan of Pat Riley's thuggish Knicks was to physically intimidate the Bulls, especially Scottie Pippen. On a late-game fast break, the Knicks' John Starks hammered Pippen to the floor, leaving him dazed and bloodied on the bench during a subsequent timeout.

I was sitting at the edge of the press table, a couple of feet from the Bulls' huddle, when Jordan shoved aside his coach, Phil Jackson, like he was the ball boy. Jordan kneeled in front of Pippen, shook a finger in his face, and snarled, "You better not take that shit," and demanded Pippen drive the ball to the rim even harder next time. In Jordan's eyes, I saw a frightening rage, however controlled, that I came to believe separated him from the others far more than his levitation skills. The old timers will tell you Bill Russell had that quality as well.

Having covered the sport from the tipoff of the rivalry between Magic Johnson and Larry Bird, right through the coming of LeBron James, I'd be the first to acknowledge that superstars drive basketball, especially the pro game, more than any other team sport. But for me, the foot soldiers and the families have always been equally and often more appealing to be around. I can still see the pride and joy on the faces of Chris Mullin's now-deceased parents, Rod and Eileen, on the day he signed his first pro contract in Oakland. I can still hear the raspy oration of Mullin's St. John's college teammate, Mark Jackson, on the sunlit Brooklyn afternoon he eulogized Harry Jackson, when he said Harry was more than a father, he was "Daddy," and everyone in the tear-stained congregation who knew the difference shouted, "Amen."

To have been a young reporter, out on the road with the Knicks, writing about people I was more used to cheering for from the Garden cheap seats, made for an unusual and unsettling transformation. Willis Reed, the captain and wounded hero of the Knicks' 1970 championship team, had replaced Holzman as coach when I began reporting in the late 1970s for the *New York Post*. Dispatched on my Murdochian mission to search and distort, I proceeded to question Reed's strategy in one of my first road games, at Cleveland. The next night, in Detroit, Reed walked into the hotel bar where I was suddenly sitting nervously, nose in my beer. He walked over, put his arm around my shoulder. "Come on over to sit with us and have something to eat," he said.

The following season, Reed was fired, the *Post*'s headline writers surely contributing, and replaced by Holzman, who remains the only Knicks coach to win a championship ring. Holzman, renowned for coaching an erudite brand of ball, was already into his sixties, but if you looked past the wrinkles, what you saw in the eyes was a street kid from Brooklyn, not so different from the African-American kids to come long after. Holzman was a tough guy with a quick needle who always got to the point. Example: When his friend and fellow basketball lifer, the Knicks' longtime scout, Fuzzy Levane, suffered a brain aneurysm and fell comatose in the early 1990s, I asked Holzman to describe Levane for a column I was preparing. It took Holzman two or three seconds to come up with the perfect quote, albeit one too colorful for the *Times:* "No one ever said, 'Here comes that asshole, Fuzzy.'"

As things would have it, Levane outlived Holzman, who died in 1998, months before his beloved Knicks made an unexpected push to the NBA finals. On the night they beat Indiana to close out the '99 Eastern Conference finals at Madison Square Garden, I bumped into Levane in a mad rush through the lower stands and up to the pressroom. He was sitting in his seat, crying. "All these nights, I've been looking across the court out of habit, to where Red always sat," he said. "I'd go home and want to tell him something about the game and I'd pick up the phone, start dialing, and say, 'What the hell am I doing?'"

Lifelong habits are tough to break, even as we lose our mentors, as the names and faces change, as the years whirl by. My father was never much of a sports fan but somehow my job covering the Knicks brought us closer than we'd ever been in the years before he died in 1990. All of a sudden, he was watching NBA games, calling me in my Brooklyn Heights apartment, making a connection. "This Larry Bird is something," he'd say. "This Bernard King . . ."

Now I watch my own sons—vertically challenged as I was—play in their youth-league games. They spend hours in the gymnasium at the local Y, they love the game, and that's all that matters. School mornings, we browse box scores over breakfast. We challenge one another in the backyard. We go see the Rutgers women play Connecticut and the preseason NIT doubleheaders at the Garden the night before Thanksgiving. We bond at night in our den, driving their mother crazy by flipping NBA League Pass channels at a furious pace, when half a dozen games are in simultaneous climax.

That's exactly where I was, reclining on the couch, watching the Knicks close out a tough road loss in Dallas, when the telephone rang on the night of November 19, 2004, the office calling to suggest that I immediately switch to ESPN. "I've never seen anything like this," the *Time*'s Sunday sports editor, Bob Goetz, said. Neither had any of us. It was sobering and sad, but as I watched those images from Auburn Hills, replayed through the night and on into the following weeks, I began to realize that they were not a chance happening, not an unavoidable car wreck, as much as they were the unfortunate culmination of events and forces that had been building for more than a decade. The veritable race riot was almost inevitable for an industry plagued by conflicts of culture and class, some of them self-created.

By conventional measures—ballooning NBA salaries, fervent corporate involvement, expanded network subsidies—it can be argued that basketball is a thriving game on both the college and pro levels. However, what are the primary indicators for whether a sport is truly succeeding? If America's universities are raking in multimillions while educating few and embarrassing many, can college basketball be worthy of applause? If the NBA is a wildly profitable vehicle for the physically blessed but reinforces stereotypes and constructs walls of alienation and mistrust, is it fulfilling its mission on a grander societal scale? Both answers are no.

The perception of basketball as a black sport over the last several decades, combined with virulent racial sensitivities in America, practically demanded that proprietary logic and good taste be maintained. They have not been. While capitalists reigned, American basketball values warped, creating a system set up to benefit those who feed off the talent more than the talented themselves. More recently, as the sport has gone global in stunningly accelerated fashion, the American system has even worked against its own players in this increasingly competitive world.

Again and again, players at both the collegiate and professional levels have made a mess of their affairs, often in painfully public ways. Too many have played the role of the jock reprobate and have been deserving of the scorn they received by the media and the fans. Here, nobody gets a free pass, but the spotlight is further cast on the powerbrokers and policy makers from the pros on down, those who turned a blind eye to the dysfunction so long as it didn't stem the flow of dollars, who could have acted a decade ago to help keep basketball a beautiful game of grace and skill, and not the ugly spectacle it turned into at The Palace of Auburn Hills.

This book, a representation of more than two decades of my covering the sport with a particular focus on my years at *The New York Times,* traces the evolutionary arc that has carried this great game to once-unimagined heights and, sadly, to alarming and dangerous depths. Using a mix of personal experience and observation in memoir form, with additional interviewing done throughout the 2004–05 season, I hope to get to the root of what has made the great American game of basketball the wonder of the world but left it stumbling at home, searching for its soul.

HARVEY ARATON
Montclair, New Jersey
Spring 2005

1

Malice

Two-and-a-half short weeks had passed since the reelection of George W. Bush. John Kerry's concession had come the morning after, leaving no hanging chads to preoccupy a country seeking domestic distraction from the calamity of the war in Iraq. Between the denouement of the brass-knuckled politics and the sudden and shocking onset of the beer-stained basketbrawl, California fertilizer salesman Scott Peterson was convicted of murdering his pregnant wife, Laci, after starring in a grim reality television series for well over a year. There was now a vacancy for generic villainy in the America's cable court of public opinion, and along came Ron Artest and a handful of relatively famous professional basketball players, all black, millionaire rich, and dragging along their entire industry to a quick, decisive, and unforgiving judgment.

It wasn't as if basketball in general and the NBA in particular were strangers to controversy and to the wrath of assorted critics nationwide. The number alone on Artest's Indiana Pacers jersey—the purposefully chosen ninety-one—evoked the contrived and inane escapades of former Chicago Bulls' bad boy Dennis Rodman. NBA-bashing, in fact, began to occur on a fairly regular basis after Michael Jordan quit the Bulls prior to the lockout-abbreviated 1998–99 season and was no longer around to obscure the collage of image-rattling headlines by heightening playoff television ratings on his way to another championship. Some of those headlines—relating to gambling bacchanals with the scent of organized crime—even involved Jordan, around the time of his 1993–94 sabbatical from the Bulls. But as long as he churned out reality television hits, as long as Jordan wielded supreme leverage with the league and enjoyed a mythic status in the media, he was untouchable, unlike those who would inherit the sport.

Preventable tragedy exacerbated a growing perception of lifestyle recklessness during the 1999–2000 season when a Charlotte Hornets' player, Bobby Phills, died in a car crash while drag-racing a teammate, David Wesley, on the road leading from the team's arena. Soon after, Jayson Williams, a retired New Jersey Nets star ensconced in an analyst's chair for network television games, was arrested in the shooting death of a chauffeur. The case involved alcohol and a nasty attempt by Williams to cover up his role in the shooting. In the summer of 2003, Kobe Bryant—the league's most luminous player, the self-styled Jordan heir—was embroiled in an explosive sexual assault case that became its own cable cause célèbre. The criminal charges were eventually dropped and a civil-suit settlement was reached, but not before Bryant's carefully crafted image as the jump-shooting boy next door was shredded and burned.

Drugs, guns, gambling, misogyny; you name it, and David Stern had been given the opportunity to explain it. After a long run of dizzying growth and critical acclaim, the longtime commissioner seemed to have a permanent place on the All-Defensive Team. His annual state of the union at the All-Star Weekend remained a spit-shined performance, replete with assurances of sustained revenue growth. But during the 2004–05 season's break in Denver, the residue of The Fight was impossible to ignore. The league announced a new fan code of conduct for its thirty arenas and implemented restrictions on alcohol consumption, including the elimination of fourth-quarter sales. (This was a wonderful and long-overdue idea, considering the number of Detroit fans whose cups were emptied on the Pacers' heads with seconds remaining in a lopsided game.)

Perhaps the most shocking and revealing development was the halftime show of the nationally televised All-Star Game. In the climate following an election supposedly won by conservatives on the moral values vote, one year after one exposed breast at the Super Bowl precipitated a near-hysterical backlash against licentiousness in the entertainment industry, the NBA even outdid the NFL's PG-rated Paul McCartney halftime bash the month before, throwing raw meat to the red-state masses. The sight of country-western singers bounding onto the court on horseback was too much for TNT commentator Charles Barkley. "This ain't no NASCAR race," complained Sir Charles, a Republican.

There was little doubt that Stern perceived the fight as a wound that needed to be salved, and fast, though in less-scripted conversation, he would ask why no one wanted to talk about the majority of NBA players who didn't show up on police dockets, or why David Robinson's $11 million largesse to create the inner-city Carver Academy school in San Antonio wasn't as big a story as Latrell Sprewell's rejection of an even larger contract extension by the Minnesota Timberwolves before the 2004–05 season. Sprewell complained to reporters that he had to feed his family but, out of touch with political correctness or good taste as he frequently was, he didn't speak for Grant Hill, any more than the conniving Bryant spoke for Tim Duncan, Allan Houston, Richard Jefferson, and dozens of others who represented the league in more conventional, stable ways.

Unfortunately for Stern, perception in the sports and entertainment business was the reality of sagging television ratings. Stern would invariably sigh when fingers were pointed, and cleverly suggest that such heated objections reflected a passion for the game. "We invite the closest view of us, and over the years, millions of fans have accepted that invitation," Stern said, when I asked him if the 2004 Christmas Day grudge match between Kobe's Lakers and Shaq's Heat misrepresented holiday values. It was one of those deflective rejoinders the lawyer in Stern was typically well prepared with, but he privately worried that a seismic event like the Pistons-Pacers brawl would make the league as toxic on Madison Avenue as it was during the late 1970s, before Stern succeeded the late Larry O'Brien as commissioner in 1984. Stern recalled the league's public image back then as "too black, too drug infested."

Over the years, Stern and I had had our squabbles, once going a couple of years without speaking, but it would have been foolish of me to let the professional relationship end and not just because Stern, as the boss of pro ball, was an important source or quote. He was also an engaging, enlightening conversationalist with much more on his mind than the state of the game. On a sports landscape mostly controlled by well-heeled Republican donors looking out for their own tax breaks, Stern steadfastly remained an active Democrat, who contributed $2,000 to the Kerry–John Edwards campaign, $25,000 to the Kerry Victory 2004 committee, and $32,500 to the Democratic Senatorial Campaign Committee. "And proud of it," he told me when I teased him following Bush's reelection about being, within the hierarchy of sports, a lone liberal wolf.

As a young man embarking on a law career, Stern did extensive pro bono work on what became a nationally renowned case challenging the unseemly practice of racial steering by real-estate brokers in and around Teaneck, the diverse northern New Jersey community in which Stern grew up. Law was his calling, until his Manhattan firm—Proskauer Rose Goetz & Mendelsohn—assigned him to its longtime NBA account. In 1978, he walked into the office of George Gallantz, his mentor, to say he had an offer from the basketball people to be legal counsel. "Well, you schmuck," Gallantz roared, "how can you put your life in the hands of one client?"

Stern rolled the dice, and became very wealthy and famous, often deified during the heady 1990s as the most savvy sports commissioner of his time, and perhaps all time. As much as Stern could make you crazy with his bullish attitudes and unfailing buoyancy, there was no doubt that he loved his league, and cared about those who passed through it. In 1986, he banished Micheal

Ray Richardson, a troubled young player with a severe stutter, for repeated drug offenses. In 2002, he quietly arranged for the Denver Nuggets to bring Richardson back into the fold, in a community-relations position.

No less a social commentator and Berkeley academic than Dr. Harry Edwards—never a wallflower when he sniffed racial injustice on the American sports scene—counted himself as an admirer, calling Stern "an honest broker of the product who, at the end of the day, respects the men who play in his league and the community from which they come." Nor was there any question that the personal and very public calamities that befell the players and increasingly alarmed the league's sponsors pained Stern to no end. He was, however, far beyond the point of cultivating himself as the friendly commissioner for all, from the wealthiest owner on down to the lowliest ball boy. The man who once dubbed himself "Easy Dave" locked out his players for much of the 1998–99 season, demanding and getting what baseball owners would die for, what sports management people called "cost certainty," in the form of a firm ceiling on salaries. On the day the lockout ended, Stern left a settlement meeting with league security on both flanks.

Given his politics and his longtime relationship with the African-American community, it was a delicate balancing act to be the top NBA cop, to operate a league that was trying, as Stern said, to "bridge both populations," the predominantly corporate crowd in the premium seats that accounted for roughly 18 percent of the league's $3 billion in revenue and the younger demographic driving the licensing and merchandising sales earning each team more than $4 million a year. Handling the fight in Auburn Hills was akin to walking the racial high wire without a net. Even as he severely punished the instigators to calm sponsors and fans, Stern was privately troubled by the belief that the behavioral bar was set higher for a league largely dominated by African-American players making huge sums of money. And who, as Stern put it, "are unencumbered by helmets, long sleeves, and pads."

This conviction was shared by many league insiders and was most strenuously articulated by Billy Hunter, the executive director of the Players Association and a former federal prosecutor, in the days following the Detroit-Indiana brawl. "I'm strongly of the opinion that a significant number of people in this country feel that most of the guys in this league don't deserve what they earn," Hunter, an African-American, told *The New York Times*. "And I think a lot of it has to do with color, with race, that the guys who are earning it are not contrite and humble enough."

While media-friendly superstars such as Magic Johnson and Michael Jordan had, for the most part, transcended racial typecasting, there was anecdotal evidence to support the opinion that Hunter wasn't just shooting from the lip, or firing up a hot air ball. Few modern athletes seemed to rouse negative emotions the way pro basketball players often could. Even in NBA fights that were confined to the court, the sight of large black men rushing off the bench to throw punches at one another tended to evoke outcries in the media and from fans about the end of sports civilization as we know it.

Wrestling is inherently violent. Real sports aren't supposed to be, but mostly white hockey crowds thrill to the sight of NHL players dropping their gloves and punching each other toothless and senseless. In 1998—about the time the combustible Sprewell was plastered in newspapers nationwide as a snarling coach-choker in cornrows following his inexcusable attack on his Golden State Warriors' coach, P. J. Carlesimo—no less a mainstream authority than *Sports Illustrated* weighed in with a sizable feature on hockey goons, extolling them as "a surprisingly honest and amiable bunch" and for abiding by the "unwritten code of the NHL tough guy." In other words, in direct opposition to the contemporary black athlete's so-called culture of disrespect, the NHL thugs comprised a laudable white, violent culture of respect.

The former was not a neighborhood that the NHL wished to wander into. In March 2000, the Florida Panthers' Peter Worrell, one of hockey's few black players, shook up the sport by failing to do what one normally does when zonked in the head with a hockey stick. As opposed to crumpling to the ice, semiconscious, oozing blood, he remained upright, alert, and enraged. Worrell responded to being attacked by the New Jersey Devils' Scott Niedermeyer with the infamous throat slash, in vogue at the time as a sort of gangsta silent battle cry, not once, twice, but three times. This infuriated the Devils and set off a leaguewide demographics alarm. While the NHL suspended Niedermeyer for ten games and did not punish Worrell, officials in the New York office were quick to make clear that such imagery had no place, and would not be tolerated, in a clean, wholesome sport like hockey.

Bobby Phills' death while drag racing David Wesley became a lesson in lifestyle recklessness. When, in 2003, Dany Heatley of hockey's Atlanta Thrashers was charged with vehicular homicide resulting in the death of his teammate, Dan Snyder, the thematic coverage focused more on Heatley's remorse and the clemency granted him by Snyder's family than on the act of driving up to eighty-two miles per hour in a thirty-five zone in Heatley's Ferrari. After all these years, such racial double standards were much too common, and mainstream sports were a powerful conditioning agent in enforcing them. In the aftermath of the Pistons-Pacers fight came the predictable dissections of the sport in print and across the airwaves, the familiar panels of blowhards hastily rounded up to outshout one another on Fox, CNN, and MSNBC. The fight was even big enough to darken the typically sanguine moods of the network morning shows.

Condemnations of the NBA's hip-hop milieu were widespread, by white and black sportswriters alike. Michael Wilbon of *The Washington Post,* Shaun Powell of *Newsday,* Bryan Burwell of the *St. Louis Post-Dispatch,* and Jason Whitlock of *The Kansas City Star*—all highly respected and African-American—railed against some black NBA players for confusing upscale basketball crowds with the audiences for rap. Whitlock warned that if the players' priorities didn't change, they'd find themselves preening for a few measly bucks on a street-ball tour, the bastardized version of the game spun off from the Harlem Rucker League and other schoolyard venues, playing to small, vociferous crowds around the country.

Watchwords like *posse*—evoking street-gang violence—crept into the postfight dialogue. Many diatribes began with "these guys," sounding too much like "black thugs with tattoos and cornrows." In my postfight column, I wondered why flamboyant hairstyles and body design, not exactly a creation of the black basketball community, were such a crime against American culture. Why were basketball players, generally speaking, the easiest targets of the sports police? Why was basketball an institution so often said to be risking ruin due to the way its players looked or comported themselves when pro football, which, in recent years, had dealt with as many, if not more, unseemly transgressions, was considered, especially as a business, the model sports league? How much of the quick-trigger and typically negative appraisals directed at Stern's "unencumbered" went only skin deep? After the column ran, Billy Hunter called to say, in so many words, "that's what I'm talking about."

On a much broader scale, it had become much too easy, almost a cliché, to blame the black athlete for diminished levels of sportsmanship and civility within the American arena. Seldom discussed was the actual genesis of disrespecting one's opponent for the benefit of self-promotion and who had established the precedent. All the way back in the 1950s, legendary Celtics coach Red Auerbach was quite good at calling attention to his own success, lighting a victory cigar on the Boston bench nearing the end of another Bill Russell–inspired victory. Auerbach's self-aggrandizements infuriated opponents, who occasionally took out their frustrations on his players. All these years later, in a climate of incivility consistently harpooned by critics, Auerbach's look-at-me revelry is still portrayed as having been part of his charisma, as good, harmless fun.

Mark Gastineau, a white defensive lineman for the Jets, was known in the 1980s for his sack dances. Long before marketing edginess became an art form, long before Dennis Rodman got his first tattoo, Jimmy Connors and then John McEnroe became the cutting edge in boorish behavior on the field of play. Their antics, ranging from playful to profane, put lily-white, country-club tennis into the mainstream conversation; tennis was said to be boring after Connors and McEnroe. A good portion of the media proceeded to habitually dismiss the all-time record-holder of grand slam titles, the gentlemanly Pete Sampras, as an unemotional serve-and-volley drone.

Media people constantly complained that basketball players were too angry. They looked too threatening, yet magazines mostly edited by middle-aged whites continuously posed them scowling on covers. Sports shows on television and radio regularly featured experts whose popularity was directly related to their ability to angrily outshout colleagues. National sports talk radio hosts tried to stir up their callers with weekly segments called *Shut Up Tuesday* and *Bite Me Wednesday.* Columnists, myself included, often fell into the trap of thinking we had to go negative to maintain a persona in the increasingly noisy chorus.

Belligerence in sports was hardly exclusive to one particular era, culture, or race. The oldtimers often made that abundantly clear whenever the serious reminiscing began. According to Dolph Schayes, the old Syracuse Nationals' star and lifelong Auerbach and Celtics hater, "Many of our games ended in fights." These days, it had just become a hell of a lot easier to promote it. Two days after what soon became known as the Malice at the Palace, Paul Silas stood outside the Cavaliers' locker room at Madison Square Garden, recalling an Atlanta night in 1968 when he and Phil Jackson got into it and Lou Hudson set the Knicks' brawny center, Willis Reed, off with a punch and, the next thing they all knew, Nate Bowman and Bill Bridges were wrestling in the stands, with Bowman, a Knick, taking a merciless pounding from the hometown fans.

"That was just one of 'em," Silas said with an unmistakable gleam in his eye. He wasn't being callous. He wasn't trying to downplay the severity of what had occurred less than forty-eight hours earlier. Silas, an NBA lifer and career-long pragmatist, was just acknowledging the realities of large, aggressive men hurling their bodies at ball and rim, battling one another on a nightly basis. There were bound to be crashes, pileups, fights, and the occasional brawl. "We'll deal with this and get past it," Silas said. "Nothing was worse than Kermit Washington and Rudy T."

Except that the 1977 punch by Washington, a Lakers' power forward shattered the face of Rudy Tomjanovich, then of the Houston Rockets, was one punch, did not involve fans, and preceded the age of cable, digital, and satellite television. Washington never quite shed the stigma of *The Punch*, the title of a later book by John Feinstein, and always believed there were racial implications of a black man nearly killing a white man. However, the episode could only be relived through grainy footage that didn't spread like a computer virus on *SportsCenter* and three hundred digital channels and the Internet. In contrast, the Pistons-Pacers game was shown live on national television and, within minutes, the fight, perfectly timed for the eleven o'clock news, transcended sports.

Even a marketing impresario like Stern, forever extracting revenue from the networks and the NBA's own channels of distribution and promotion, was stunned by how the medium could, in a heartbeat, become a deadly energy source, a near-nuclear meltdown. "They just show it and show it and show it," he told me, exasperated, acknowledging that the fight had become the Zapruder film of sports. In the hours following the debacle, he watched it dozens of times, every horrific frame, beginning with Artest's cheap foul on Detroit's Ben Wallace in the final minute of a lopsided Indiana victory.

Lost on Artest, apparently, was the well-known fact that Wallace happened to be mourning the death of his oldest brother. Artest offered his sympathy by hammering the bigger man, and one he wasn't even guarding, as Wallace drove by. It wasn't the worst foul the flagrantly aggressive Artest had ever committed, but it had to rank in his top five of most unnecessary, and just to make sure Wallace knew who had sent him to the floor, Artest held his position, making himself readily available for Wallace to respond.

The action escalated quickly. Wallace choke-shoved Artest backward, Artest retreated like Ali, fake-wobbling into the ropes. Players spilled onto the court, Artest settled back into a reclining position on the press table—a bizarre, Rodmanian act in its own right. That Artest would instigate a scuffle with Wallace, a ferocious competitor but respected as a clean player and a gentleman, was bad enough, but when a cup of beer or soda (not a bottle, as was often reported) flew out of the stands and landed on his chest (not his face, as was often reported), Artest bolted from the table and, in one fateful moment, touched off a riot that, as Stern put it, broke "the social contract between players and fans."

Stern knew these subsequent, sad, and crystal-clear color images would be most haunting. The well-traveled Pacers guard, Stephen Jackson, followed Artest into the stands for no rational reason and began swinging at fans. Jermaine O'Neal rushed twenty feet across the court to lay one out with a roundhouse right. A metal chair flew into the crowd. A young boy, eyes filled with fright, sobbed as a woman held him close. Pacers players, in the process of being led off by team personnel, their jerseys stretched or torn, were drenched in beverage showers, all of this madness eventually bringing criminal assault charges against five players and five fans, and an 871-page report by the Auburn Hills police.

In the report, first obtained by *The Detroit News*, Pacers' coach Rick Carlisle blamed the Pistons, the team that had fired him during the summer of 2003, for lax security and the Pistons' coaches for failing to hustle Wallace from the floor after he became incensed. "Ben threw his towel and that was the cue to start throwing things at Ron [Artest]," Carlisle told investigators.

Even taking team alliances and biases into consideration, it was amazing that anyone could try to absolve Artest of guilt, much less of the majority of it. Two incidents had occurred: the Artest-Wallace encounter that seemed to be under control until the thrown cup hit Artest, and the ensuing riot. Artest had instigated both. "Ben had blocked his shot a couple of minutes before the fight, and Artest cursed him," said then-Pistons coach Larry Brown, Carlisle's replacement in this tangled rivalry of 2004 Eastern Conference playoff finalists (the Pistons beat the Pacers on their way to the championship).

The fight was especially painful for Brown, whose eleven-year-old son, L.J., was a ball boy that night at the far end of the floor, by the Indiana bench. "He doesn't even want to go to the game anymore," confided Brown, an emotional five-nine scrapper from Long Island who seldom backed away from any confrontation, from his days as an All-America point guard at North Carolina to beating his hard head against the wall as Allen Iverson's caretaker and 76ers coach in Philadelphia. Brown, naturally, had a completely different take than Carlisle as to what might have prevented the fight from spilling into the stands, and shared it one night at Madison Square Garden as the Pistons were warming up.

"Artest is such a tough guy and he commits a foul like that in the last minute of a game they're beating the heck out of us," Brown said. "If he wanted to fight Ben, why was he backing away? Ben would have settled it right there and none of the other stuff would have happened."

Stern didn't have the luxury of dealing with the hypothetical. By the following morning, he knew he had to move expeditiously, or risk aftershocks. He didn't even bother to wait for the work week to begin, calling a news conference before the Knicks-Cavaliers Sunday night game at the Garden. Just as Silas happened to be revisiting the 1968 Atlanta brawl in the hallway by the visiting locker room, Stern passed by, the top of his white shirt unbuttoned, his tie undone. In the more than twenty-five years of running into him at one NBA event or another, I had never seen him grimmer.

He appeared alone at the press conference, as if to stress the point that the major suspensions—the season for Artest, thirty-five games for Stephen Jackson, and twenty-five for O'Neal—were not communally inspired. Asked if there had been a vote, Stern nodded, with a glower befitting his surname. "One–nothing," he said. Off to the side of the podium, Charles Smith, a former Knick and longtime union activist, winced when he heard the news. Jamison Brewer, a Knicks' reserve guard who was Artest's friend when he played for the Pacers, called the suspension crazy, and said most players in Artest's position would have reacted likewise. Even Silas commented that Artest should have been given some credit for backing away from Wallace and minding his own business on the press table. Many players around the league would say they might well have reacted the way Artest had if hit with a flying object from the stands. Charles Barkley, a veteran of more than a few embarrassing scraps during his playing days, argued in various interviews that it was a player's right to pursue any miscreant who used him for target practice, social contract be damned.

Stern wasn't hearing any of it, citing Artest's long list of prior transgressions as reason enough to throw the book at him. Artest, who turned twenty-five six days before the fight, had been fined and suspended repeatedly for various offenses during his five seasons with the Bulls and Pacers. In the ensuing days and weeks, many basketball-savvy sources whose opinions I often sought out told me they thought Stern had overreacted, that strong suspensions were warranted but that these were too severe. One of them, however, wasn't Harry Edwards. "First of all, any player who goes into the stands is stupid, especially for a person whose livelihood depends on his body staying in one piece," Edwards said. He, better than most, understood the racial complexities in play for the commissioner, the revenue for all being risked, the unenviable position Stern found himself in, between a couple of rockheaded players and his fan base. "What is going to happen and what will people say the next time someone goes into the stands and gets stabbed?" Edwards said. "Stern is looking to say, 'Listen, fellas, for the sake of the league, for your own sake, this is what's going to happen if you go into the stands.' "

Hunter, the union executive director, challenged the severity of the suspensions and Stern's ability to unilaterally impose them. In the cases of Artest and Jackson, which he lost, I didn't agree. Jackson had no excuse, no reason to be in the stands. Artest, for his part, attacked the wrong fan (and, tellingly, one with a cup in his hand). When Artest expressed his remorse on *Good Morning America* by pitching an R&B CD he'd produced (and had, shortly before the fight, asked for time off to promote), there was only one conclusion to draw: Here was a young man who had no concept of accountability, who needed time off for his own benefit, as much as for those whose lives he had continually disrupted.

More of a dilemma was voicing approval for the twenty-five games off given O'Neal, a twenty-six-year-old All-Star, who responded to seeing a teammate, Anthony Johnson, on the ground, by barreling across the floor, sliding on his butt, and cold-cocking a fan. The fan, Charlie Haddad, was out on the court, where he didn't belong, but already in the grasp of security. In the heat of the riot, O'Neal said it felt like "us against the world, twelve guys in Pacers' jerseys against thousands."

In several ways, some superficial, O'Neal fit the unflattering stereotype of the young, so-called hip-hop generation player. He braided his hair and sported a multitude of tattoos, extending from both muscular shoulders down to his forearms. As a high-school junior in Columbia, South Carolina, he was found in bed with his fifteen-year-old girlfriend and sweated out an investigation that could have led to charges of statutory rape. O'Neal skipped college and was drafted right onto the roster of the Portland Trail Blazers. He proceeded to ride the bench and was labeled a flop, an anti-Kobe. Back home in Columbia following his rookie year, he had a scuffle with a mall security guard and wound up digging ditches and picking up garbage to complete 100 hours of community service.

After four years and little opportunity, O'Neal was dispatched to Indiana, in a deal for Dale Davis, a veteran forward. The trade immediately became one of the worst in NBA history. Pacers' CEO Donnie Walsh took a look at O'Neal during the Pacers' training camp and thought he was too good to be true. He was an intimidating presence on defense. He had natural low-post skills and was that rarity among American-trained big men in that he could step outside the paint and launch feathery jump shots. Walsh thought there had to have been some problem with this kid. The better O'Neal played, the more Walsh worried and waited for "the other shoe to drop." It didn't. O'Neal became an All-Star and was selected for the U.S. National team in the 2002 World Championships in Indianapolis. He became the Pacers' captain.

Larry Bird, the team's president of basketball operations, called O'Neal the "cornerstone of the franchise" when he signed a new contract during the summer of 2003. Typically well dressed in public, articulate in interviews, O'Neal cultivated a philan-thropic presence in the Indianapolis community. He launched a foundation and forged a partnership with an Indianapolis hospi-tal, St. Vincent's. After the devastating tsunami hit south Asia, O'Neal announced he would donate a thousand dollars for every point he scored in his next game. He scored 32 and then decided to base his gift on his previous game's total: 55.

O'Neal focused much of his philanthropic works on the Indi-anapolis Housing Authority. He annually donated $25,000 to fund a Christmas toy drive, another $25,000 for clothes. He initi-ated a program for strengthening father-son relationships by sponsoring nights out at the Pacers' games. Working with the local housing authority was important to him, he said, because he had grown up in the projects, abandoned by his father just before birth.

Prior to Christmas and the Pacers' first game against the Pis-tons since the fight, O'Neal had his suspension reduced from twenty-five games to fifteen by an NBA arbitrator on internal NBA labor-management disputes, Roger Kaplan. Cited was O'Neal's work in the community, his positive image. Stern challenged the decision, losing in federal court, on December 30, when the Pacers were in the New York area for a game against New Jersey.

Dressed in a cream-colored three-piece suit, O'Neal held an impromptu news conference outside the locker room and was asked if he felt vindicated. He shook his head. Punishment had been warranted. "There is really no vindication for the fans and players involved," he said. "Vindication means there was no wrong and this was wrong." He was still facing two counts of aggravated assault in Auburn Hills, Michigan, but was relieved that the arbitrator reduced the suspension and had specifically mentioned his community work. His concern was that he, as a young black male who was trying to be a positive community role model, would be superficially judged.

"People say the league is too hip-hop, too out of control," O'Neal said. "I don't understand that. I have tattoos but I care about people. I love my daughter." In fact, he said the worst moment of the entire episode was when five-year-old Asjia came home from school and said, "Daddy, you only threw one punch." He was sorry for it all, and was the only player to make a heartfelt apology to "all the fans and the people who are not necessarily fans of the NBA that they even had to watch something like that."

However, O'Neal recognized the hypocrisy, the shifting standards, the complexity of the rap culture that, in part, did promote violence and misogyny but whose audience included swaths of white suburbia. He wondered why heavy-metal music wasn't an issue when white athletes—hockey or baseball players—brawled. He wanted to know how many men his age of any job or race were expected to act like a Cub Scout 24/7. He couldn't. He wouldn't. Back with his teammates in the locker room, O'Neal removed his sports jacket and hung it on a hook. He began bantering with the Pacers' New York City–bred point guard, Jamal Tinsley, who asked him if he'd had to speak at the hearing.

O'Neal sneered. "Man," he said, stretching out the word, "I just wanted to tell the judge, 'This is bullshit.'"

In the time it had taken to walk through the locker-room door, O'Neal had dropped his polished public persona. But was this unscripted moment, this look inside the jock cocoon, so different from what we would see peaking inside any exclusive male sanctum? In the golfers' private areas at Augusta? The back rooms of Congress? O'Neal was in his element, his neighborhood, sounding young and mutinous. He would soon go on a scoring tear, about which he would say: "I've been almost angry to a point, just angry. Sometimes anger makes me play even better, makes me play harder." In other words: on the edge.

About the time I spoke with Harry Edwards, a new documentary by Ken Burns on the legendarily controversial boxer Jack Johnson had debuted on PBS. Burns called it *Unforgivably Black*, and Edwards believed the title was especially relevant to the contemporary young African-American basketball stars. "Jack Johnson was the father of the athlete for today," Edwards said. "His attitude was, 'Hey, this is who I am.' Obviously, for Ron Artest and Jermaine O'Neal to be spoken of in the same breath doesn't make any sense, except that they are part of the same culture. And that's what basketball is dealing with, a whole spectrum of kids who belong to a different generation, young men who are going to braid their hair and wear tattoos and not apologize for it because they think they're being true to where they are from. But to a lot of the fans out there, it's a representation of something bad, something threatening. Today it's Ron Artest, tomorrow it could be LeBron James."

When I was a young Knicks beat reporter for the *New York Post* in 1979, the team fielded its first all-black roster, and an early season meeting with the Detroit Pistons was the first game in NBA history without a single white player. I wrote that it was an important social achievement for African-Americans but also a watershed development that Americans were by and large too enlightened to fear. All good intentions aside, I should have been whistled for flagrant naïveté. Then, as now, pro basketball's blackness was always a major component in how the league was promoted, received, and, ultimately, judged. Race was the elephant in the arena, the microcosm of the society at large, whether people were willing to see it or not.

For some, it was tempting to use the race card speciously, even recklessly, as when Phoenix point guard Steve Nash, a white Canadian, edged out Shaquille O'Neal, on merit, in the 2005 most valuable player polling of selected media members. For others, the subject was too much a conundrum, too threatening, and better dealt with in corporate-speak, or with demographic contrivances, if not in outright denial.

This was where Stern, the straight and narrow CEO, typically outmuscled Stern, the progressive thinker. With the suspensions meted out, the games rolling on, Stern ignored Billy Hunter's calls for open, honest dialogue. He got on the telephone from his Colorado vacation home and called the Auburn Hills debacle the work of "fifteen fans and five players." He added, "We should be judged by our response to it and let's move on." But insisting that the fight was just a one-time event—"the perfect storm," he said—was no way to acknowledge the mistakes and missteps made by the NBA in particular and the basketball industry at large that had helped create the conditions for the chaos to volcanically erupt.

The sport, unfortunately, had been belching the residue of its shortsighted money-grabbing for the better part of a decade. People I have known for many years who were at The Palace of Auburn Hills that night spoke of the anger in the air, palpable and ugly, a gladiatorial ambiance that over the years had become pervasive in too many NBA arenas. Obviously this was partly attributable to the intensity between two physical rivals, but it was more a by-product of a regrettable marketing scheme to create an in-your-face product that was edgy enough to resonate with the young and rebellious, those who would buy the jerseys, play the video games, create the buzz.

However, the fans paying a king's ransom for the expensive seats were much less forgiving, more easily antagonized upon the sounding of those deep-rooted racial alarms. Drunk or not, too many basketball fans had reached the point where they objectified the players, could not relate to them as human beings, or see beyond societal stereotypes and flimsily disguised racial codes. If the imagery of large black men beating on defenseless white fans was alarming, the too-widely accepted pastime of affluent whites feeling empowered to verbally abuse half-dressed, sweaty black men should have evoked even more discomfort and disturbing American historical chapters.

The irony was that, the more the fans shelled out for their seats, the closer they got to the action—but the closer they got, the wider the gulf between them and players seemed to grow. The arguments over which side of the basketball divide was more to blame could be carried on ad infinitum, but, when all was said and done, the sad spectacle revealed more about how American big business operated, more about profiteering than it did about punches, more about how gluttonous corporations had steered the sport off course and over time created a powder keg ready to blow on a short racial fuse.

2

Changing Times

IN 1992, just weeks before embarking on a marketing extravaganza that would rock the Olympics and launch the reconfiguration of the basketball-playing world, the NBA lost one of its pioneers and symbolically buried its more modest past. With that year's postseason underway, an irascible Italian immigrant named Daniel Biasone died of cancer at eighty-three. Most NBA players couldn't have told you who Biasone was if a season's worth of paychecks depended on it, but they owed him plenty, at the very least a vigorous nod of thanks. Basketball, invented by James Naismith, was in 1954 reinvented by Biasone, owner of the long-defunct Syracuse Nationals and the unquestioned father of the 24-second shot clock.

Part of his inspiration grew out of his hatred for Red Auerbach and the Boston Celtics, out of watching his players chase the globe-trotting Bob Cousy around the court, to no avail. "They had Cousy, who was the best dribbler," Biasone said in an interview a year before his death. "One time, they're beating us by a point with about eight minutes left. So Red gives the ball to Cousy, and they go into a stall. Would you believe that neither team took a shot for that whole last eight minutes? I said to Red right then, 'We gotta have a time clock.' But he was with the guys who didn't want it—because he had Cousy."

Biasone, a member of the league's rules committee, continued to badger anyone and everyone, warning that a game lacking in time limits of possession would never last, much less grow. He intensified his efforts after a March 21, 1953, playoff game when Cousy scored 50 points against the Nationals, 30 of them on free throws. This was probably the game still gnawing at Biasone many years later, claiming it was so dull that many fans walked out. Eventually, enough league owners listened to him, and adopted a formula that had been devised by Biasone's general manager, Leo Ferris: the 2,880 seconds of a 48-minute game divided by the average number of shots a game over the previous three seasons (120). Biasone finally won the argument and, inadvertently, wound up defeating himself.

While scoring increased by an average of 14 points per game during the 1954–55 season, proving Biasone's point, it was Auerbach who soon landed Bill Russell. Nobody could trigger the fast break like the dominant big man and that was the perfect weapon in a faster, more eye-catching game. When the Celtics began stockpiling championship upon championship, Auerbach began getting the credit for revolutionizing the sport. Biasone, forever steaming in Syracuse, soon began to be viewed as an anachronism, as an impediment to a more lucrative future for all.

Nobody much liked going to Syracuse, a cold outpost in winter, and one of the last small industrial markets, such as Rochester and Fort Wayne. Auerbach used the threat of longer Syracuse layovers to motivate his players, promising dinners of cold Chinese takeout. From the mid-1950s and, especially after the Lakers moved from Minneapolis to Los Angeles in 1961, teams such as Boston and New York pushed Biasone hard to move west, to San Francisco, the way baseball's Giants followed its Dodgers. Biasone burned when Ned Irish of the Knicks would say: "What does Syracuse versus New York look like on the Madison Square Garden marquee?"

Biasone wasn't about to leave Syracuse or the Eastwood Sports Center, the bowling alley from which he ran his beloved

Nats. In the bar, Biasone's players would drink and be merry, or melancholy, long into the night after their games at the State Fair Coliseum and later the Syracuse War Memorial. Biasone, all five feet, six inches of him, relished being the league's feisty little guy. He turned a deaf ear on pleas to surrender Syracuse. He held on as long as he could, appointing himself assistant coach when the league ruled the bench off-limits to owners. He forged close relationships with the players as if they were the children he and his wife never had. He lived and died with their successes and failures, showing up at the airport in a snowstorm one night after his team returned from a painful defeat. "Can't we beat anyone?" he asked, hat all covered with snow, as his players filed silently past.

Biasone finally gave up in 1963, sold the Nationals and watched them move to Philadelphia, where they became the 76ers. Time stood still inside the Eastwood Sports Center, on the picture-filled walls and trophy-laden shelves of Biasone's tiny office. A couple of weeks before they would be pallbearers at his funeral, two Nationals' stars, Dolph Schayes and Paul Seymour, visited Biasone at the old haunt. They shared lunch. They traded war stories. They talked about how big and successful the league had gotten after more than a decade of Magic, Larry, and then Michael. "He always felt that the league shouldn't grow on the back of the average fan, but that's exactly what had happened," Schayes said. "Danny was saying that the average guy can't even afford to go to a game anymore. That really bothered him. Danny was always for the little guy."

By 1992, professional basketball was already far from its lunch-pail roots. Corporations were clamoring to get on board. Following steady growth through the 1980s, league revenues were surging at the rate of 20 percent a year. Especially in the major markets, the NBA game was increasingly becoming a place to be seen. Up in Syracuse, Biasone watched this televised pageantry, still passionate as ever about the game, complaining from his deathbed at the University Hospital in Syracuse to the visiting Schayes that that the hospital wasn't wired for cable during the

NBA playoffs. He nonetheless was uneasy with the direction of the sport, with its then $300 front-row seats with waiter service, with its obsession for tax-funded arenas with hundreds of luxury boxes. What were these people attending—a basketball game or a four-star restaurant? Something just didn't feel right about this new era of opulence. Biasone, the shot-clock visionary, had another premonition. "The bubble's going to burst," he told Dolph Schayes. "Just you wait."

What would Danny Biasone have said more than a dozen years later, watching the lunacy unfold at The Palace of Auburn Hills? Would it have struck a nostalgic chord, reminded him of old-time brawls at the War Memorial? Would he have placed the blame on the offending players and a couple of suburban Detroit fans later reported to have histories of criminal behavior? Or would he have examined the American basketball industry at large and been troubled by a much deeper crisis? Would the twenty-first century television ratings for the NBA Finals, more or less half what they'd been during the Jordan era, have him gloating to the bowling-alley regulars that he'd seen it coming from the start? And what would he say about this new breed of fan, who, when push came to punch, proved not to be much of a sports fan at all?

The Pacers' CEO, Donnie Walsh, who played his college ball at North Carolina and spent much of his life around basketball crowds, argued that loud, taunting fans were nothing new and were logically endemic to the sport, given their close proximity to the court. "When we played at Duke, the students were doing the heckling, the jumping up and down, back then," Walsh said. And, of course, the years when the southern schools were desegregating, when black players began showing up, one by one, were no love-ins, either. But, yes, Walsh admitted, these days too often seemed like those days. The heckling had grown angrier, especially at the professional level, much more personal. "It's gotten far worse the last few years in the NBA," he said.

He would know, since the Pacers' fans, first at Market Square Arena and more recently at Conseco Fieldhouse, were considered to be among the worst in the league. Throughout the 1990s, when the Pacers had a fierce playoff rivalry with the Knicks, fans would scream foul, racist remarks at Patrick Ewing, Anthony Mason, and John Starks from the vicinity of the visitors' bench. In the heat of the game and occasionally in its aftermath, the players would yell right back. Reporters from the New York media would sit along the baseline, within earshot, and, in retrospect, must understand that a Palace-like conflagration might have broken out on any number of occasions. In this heartland of family values, many fans seemed to check theirs at the door. Around the country, red state or blue, it could be just as bad. "People are coming now with the attitude that you can sit there and yell anything, things they would never yell to someone across the street," Walsh said.

Stern agreed that fans were going too far. They were taking liberties they wouldn't have years ago. But wasn't that happening everywhere? Wasn't indecency rampant in our entertainment culture? At most sporting venues? Weren't parents punching each other out on the sidelines of the their kids' soccer and hockey games? The NBA environment, he said, was merely "a reflection of the culture." But that explanation failed to address and define the league's role and its responsibilities in creating a more civil atmosphere inside its arenas, and one that spared no effort to guarantee protection and encourage sensitivity.

Too often fans failed to distinguish between the basketball game and a night out at the bar. Until the NBA finally acted with its new alcohol policy announced at the 2005 All-Star Game in Denver, here was an example of an industry-wide complicity, or irresponsibility, and why Stern's "reflection of the culture" refrain ultimately was a partial forfeiture of responsibility.

There were other, less obvious, ways for the NBA, in trying to broaden its appeal, to wade into turbulent social waters. Take the case of America West Arena in Phoenix, a league venue where the crowd was overwhelmingly white, and where the Suns' mascot had long been a bloke dressed in a gorilla suit. Black players had been passing through for years and wondering, as union executive director Billy Hunter said, "What a gorilla has to do with the Valley of the Sun?" as the area around Phoenix is called. In 1999, this at-best cheesy act went too far when Oliver Miller, whose well-publicized weight problems had all but destroyed a once-promising career, came to town with the Sacramento Kings. In front of a sellout crowd that included his in-laws and children, Miller was cruelly parodied by the court jester in the gorilla suit, who stuffed a tube under his costume to dramatically increase his girth, donned a Miller jersey, pretended to gorge himself on popcorn, and then fell to the floor, unable to get up.

The tape of the incident showed Miller looking on, practically in shock. His agent would later claim that a subsequent binge, which forced Miller off the Kings' active roster, was the result of this sad spectacle. The Suns apologized for Miller being "affected detrimentally," but justified the routine by calling it "one in a long line of eighteen years' worth of parodies of coaches and players performed by the premier mascot in all of team sports."

It would have been bad enough had the Suns' mascot been a duck who tried to humiliate a man struggling, quite painfully and visibly, with an eating disorder. Hunter watched the crowd whoop it up over the depiction of a troubled player as a "fat, lazy ape" and, with good reason, saw something much worse. "Because of the history of this country, because blacks have historically been portrayed as monkeys and apes, not only did they disparage Oliver but they disparaged me and, based on what a lot of players have told me, a lot of other people in our league," he said.

Even Stern somehow missed this point. In a law-and-order league in which a player could be fined for wearing his shorts south of the knee, the Suns were not punished, or even ordered to retire the Gorilla. The fans liked him. The media—*Sports Illustrated*'s popular columnist Rick Reilly included—celebrated him. Along with the laser shows, the fireworks, the busty dancers, the clattering scoreboards, and the screaming public address announcers, the Gorilla was part of what the NBA considered the total game experience, and one that had grown more mindless and increasingly interactive.

Shortly after the fight at The Palace of Auburn Hills, my friend Michelle Musler, a long-time Knicks' season-ticket holder who, for many years, has been ensconced in the first row directly behind the Knicks bench, forwarded me a brochure she had recently received, pitching unsold tickets for the remainder of the 2004–05 season. On the cover was the team's point guard, Stephon Marbury, with Madison Square Garden silhouetted in the background and the following recruiting pitch printed in white, block letters: TOUGH. AGGRESSIVE. FEARLESS. Flip the brochure open and the punch line was delivered: AND THAT'S JUST THE FANS.

This particular group was presented in full color, in a striking this-could-be-you pose, in midgame frenzy, faces contorted, mouths open, fists clenched. In other words, ready to rumble. Am I claiming that the Knicks or any other NBA team were encouraging people to come to the game and get into a fight? Of course not, but the marketing too often sounded like a none-too-subtle invitation to come be the proverbial sixth man, disruptively loud, selectively rude. Or what Michelle had been complaining about to me for several years: the embarrassingly capricious nature of a crowd once celebrated for its sophistication and understanding of the game. She hated it when they screamed profanity at the players, or jeered the minute the Knicks fell behind in a game, as if they were cattle in need of prodding.

She had come to the conclusion that too many people of this upscale NBA audience attended the game now believing that heckling the players was part of the fun and often the point. It was their privilege, their right, and, what the hell? They were paying small fortunes for their tickets, or at least their company was. The players were making millions they didn't deserve. Mix these attitudes with alcohol, especially in the case of the younger male demographic, and what you had was a rowdier, less-savvy crowd that too often wouldn't know Oscar Robertson from Oscar Meyer.

Moreover, the target audience was narrowing because most fans just couldn't afford these prices. The aforementioned Knicks' brochure was pitching tickets ranging from $240 to $728 each. While the average NBA ticket for the 2004–05 season was a shade more than $45, according to calculations by the Chicago-based *Team Marketing Report*, the cost for an average family of four to attend a game, factoring in parking and food, was a league-average $263. For a premium ticket, the average was $153.80 (with the average ticket topping out at $416 in Houston and a low of $90 in Oakland, where the Golden State Warriors play). "The real fans," as Michelle referred to the sect in which she proudly included herself, were being priced out.

I have known Michelle for about a quarter of a century and believe she is one of those special people who make a professional sport succeed, often despite itself. She had a run of ten years when she missed only one Knicks home game. Occasionally she blew off a preseason game, but you could always count on Michelle, her bag of daily newspapers at her side, showing up on game night, even more than you could the Knicks. A reporter covering the team got to know her like he got to know the coach.

We met in 1981 at the NBA All-Star Game in Cleveland, which that year was played at the old Richfield Coliseum, a distant suburban arena that seemed to appear, out of nowhere, like a giant moon base after a monotonous drive across the bland northern Ohio plain. As she often did, Michelle scored tickets from her league contacts and flew in for the weekend. I was working at the time for the *New York Post*, covering the Knicks. Michelle introduced herself at a media reception, saying she was a fan, a regular reader of my stories.

A single mother of five, whose adult children were closer in age to me than she was, Michelle gradually became a close friend, a confidant, a part-time shrink, and continues in these roles. She listened sympathetically to my sad twentysomething tales of neurotic relationships with women and enthusiastically to my insider's tales of the locker room. The irony was that Michelle often knew as much about the inner workings of the Knicks as I did, if not more. She was my eyes and ears around the Knicks' bench. In Charley O's, the now displaced restaurant and watering hole on the Garden's Thirty-first Street side, she was my entrée to the world of players' wives and girlfriends (in some awkward cases, one of each per player). Even the gossipy *Post* couldn't handle some of the material coming out of those late-night huddles.

The 1981 Cleveland All-Star Game is best remembered for a massive ice storm that rolled into town, making for a miserable and dangerous bus ride for the entire NBA contingent to Richfield. It could be argued, retrospectively, that the weather gods were punishing the league for deserting the city, where the game belonged, in a misguided attempt to market itself as a more upscale sport. The Cavaliers, who later returned to the new Gund Arena in downtown Cleveland, weren't the only urban deserters of that era.

In February 2005, *The New York Times,* in a story about Detroit's shrinking population and city services, reported that 15,168 businesses had left the Motor City since 1972. One of the earliest and most historically significant to flee was Detroit's pro basketball team. Hockey's Red Wings remained in town, flourishing at the downtown Joe Louis Arena. Baseball's Tigers built a new stadium in the city near the turn of the century. Football's Lions even returned from the suburbs. Bill Davidson, the Pistons' owner, insisted that basketball, the city game, would die in Detroit. In 1978, the Pistons packed up from the old downtown Cobo Arena and fled to an antiseptic domed football stadium in Pontiac. They eventually settled into The Palace of Auburn Hills, far, far away from urban blight, from the predominantly African-American city. When the Pistons built a winner around the effervescent Isiah Thomas and became NBA champions in 1989, there was no easy access to these black icons for fans from Detroit. There was no mass transit, only a long, tangled commute on Interstate 75.

Several years ago, I ran into Dave Bing, the great shooting guard who carried the Pistons from 1966 through 1975, was elected to the Hall of Fame in 1990, and was named one of the NBA's fifty greatest players by the league for a fifty-year anniversary promotion in 1996. When his playing days were over, Bing, a Washington, D.C., native, settled in Detroit. He got into the steel business and eventually became one of the city's leading manufacturers, operating five downtown plants, creating badly needed jobs.

Bing believed it was a tragedy that the Pistons left Detroit. For the young, black male, those players became more untouchable, more unlikely to step into their neighborhoods, their community centers. "From all my years at Cobo, I got to know all these people who were kids when I was playing and now I know them thirty, forty years," he said. Some of them Bing eventually put to work. "One relationship leads to another," he said, "but it all depends on accessibility, and now we live in a city where the game is so far away from the kids."

And that was where the so-called Detroit Pistons were when push came to shove and eventually to shame. The Palace was in the middle of a giant parking lot, surrounded by stretches of highway and back roads leading to posh suburban enclaves. If the NBA's global marketing miracle had finally come to face the fragile rapport it had developed with its core audience in the United States, it could be said that this was the appropriate setting to look in the mirror, to face up to its manifest sense of upward mobility. Of course, there were other means of forcing separation from the working- and middle-class audiences the NBA had played to in less heady times, all the way back to the days of Danny Biasone. All a team had to do was gentrify those neighborhoods in their arena with the best views of the court, one by one, set the rich conveniently apart from the rabid riffraff.

Even factoring for inflation, it was difficult to fathom what many of these tickets cost, how much some people were willing to pay for forty-eight basketball minutes. When Michelle bought her first courtside season ticket, she paid $14 per game. By 1998, it was $220 a pop. By the 2004–05 season, it was $330, raised once again, despite the Knicks' languid play since the turn of the century. Once every spring, in fact, Michelle informs me she has received her invoice for her season's tickets and will be promptly faxing it along to me, as an expression of exasperation. She typically includes the welcome-back letter, most years indignantly taking the time to scrawl in the margin: "No reference to price increase." She admits, "I'm embarrased to tell people what I pay for basketball tickets," and over the years, her children have become increasingly intolerant of her complaints, knowing she would inevitably write the check anyway.

When, they wondered, would she outgrow this draining obsession? On the far side of sixty-five, Michelle's business slowed during the economic downturn. She, like so many others, took a stock-market hit. She had downsized, selling her spacious home in a wooded cul-de-sac and moving into a condo in downtown Stamford, Connecticut. All around Michelle, faces in the stands were changing. The "real fans" were leaving. So many people from her section had gone home to watch on television, or not at all, the ultimate payback. Like Dennis, the postal worker who brought priests from his community, and Danny, who though legally blind knew more about basketball than anyone Michelle knew, including me. Her friends from down the row, the Coplands and the Tamans, were told by the man who'd sold them tickets for twenty years to get lost when he realized he could extract a lot more from brokers than he could from them.

Market logic suggested the clamor for premium seats would have quieted or the prices flattened out as the Knicks' fortunes sagged following a lengthy run in the 1990s under coaches Pat Riley and then Jeff Van Gundy as a quality team. Their years-long string of sellouts was over. Though the league proudly announced it had set an all-time attendance record in 2004–05, a season when it expanded to thirty teams, many teams were known to be creative in the calculation of attendance figures for public consumption. Arenas around the country that once routinely played to capacity had chunks of brightly colored empty seats that were impossible to miss while watching on television, as the ball moved up and down the court.

This was the NBA conundrum, what to do when those court-side tickets, raised again and again to cash in on demand, became less attractive in cities where once-formidable teams had declined. Stern and many owners often rationalized the cost by comparing an NBA game to a Broadway show, but as Fred Klein, a longtime Knicks fan, said, "If an NBA team stinks, they don't shut down the production and give your money back."

Klein had seen his share of beautiful and bad basketball at the Garden, missing only thirty-two games over forty-five years. The one-time owner of the famous Carnegie Deli and his buddy, Stan Asofsky, had been living and dying with the Knicks from front-row seats along the baseline, since 1959, after meeting at a basketball game as opponents at Manhattan's Ninety-second Street Y. Klein had heard that Asofsky was a dirty player and decided to make a stand early. "I punched him," he said. "We had a fight." They became close friends, moved their act downtown to the Garden, acted out their aggressions by baiting the refs. Fred and Stan's seats once cost $2.50 and were now $240, getting a break for the obstructed view behind the basket. "Used to be the respect for the sport was much greater," Fred said. "You had people who loved the game. You had the gamblers who lived and died on every play. Now it's more of a fashion show. It's not the same feeling."

Asofsky wasn't coming as much, selling off games to defray the cost, a strategy Michelle flirted with, though she feared the moment she walked away and severed her ties, the Knicks would swing a huge deal, luck into another Patrick Ewing, become contenders again. She still loved the action from close up, at least when the everchanging Knicks' coach (Larry Brown for the 2005–06 season) wasn't giving her a $330 view of the back of his head. She looked forward to dinner with one of her friends who rotated on her second ticket, or spoiling one of her three grand-children with the best seats a kid could have.

The Garden didn't feel the same, not as homey as it used to be. She would gladly have traded the waiter service for the old days, when players and coaches would turn around and chat, and when many even knew her name. Michelle acknowledged she might be too old-fashioned, or "just too old," but she stubbornly clung to the conviction that this new generation of courtside fan—bringing unhealthy attitudes about players to the game and feeling entitled to express them given the cost of the ticket—was a major part of what ailed the sport. She cursed under her breath when the profanities rained down from a few rows behind her. She rolled her eyes when one of the unfamiliar faces whipped out a cell phone and started dialing the world. "The kind of fan who is yelling, 'Turn on the television, look where I'm sitting,'" she said. The kind more interested in Celebrity Row directly across the floor, where Spike Lee held court.

Over the years, Lee had taken a few hits as something of a publicity hound. He was even blamed for a 1994 Knicks playoff loss after Reggie Miller erupted in the fourth quarter, claiming he'd been inspired by Lee. But those of us who were around the Garden before Lee became a famous film director remembered him dodging ushers, working his way courtside to chat with players and reporters, only to be escorted to the ramp and back upstairs to his nosebleed seat. By Michelle's and anyone's honest standards, Lee was a "real fan," and at least he reportedly paid for his tickets, not like the freeloading stars who routinely dropped in, on the house, hoping to land the next morning in the tabloid gossip pages. Not that Knicks management minded. The celebrities made the paying saps think they were attending something important, even when the game turned out to be a formless dud.

It was a mutually beneficial synergy and crossmarketing spectacle, the rich and famous obliterating the already blurred lines between entertainment and sports. While New York and Los Angeles obviously had the most celebrities to strut, all NBA markets had their share of VIPs, their local business poobahs, to practically plop into the laps of the players, forever improvising ways to extract premium revenue from every inch of available space. "What can I do?" Stern said when I raised the question of fans getting too close for their own safety and the players' security. "The owners want to make money."

Admittedly, sportswriters, myself included, weren't keen on the prospect of completely losing their own courtside views and ability to write intimately about the game. It was bad enough covering football games from the sterility of a press box in the sky. Basketball was a last stronghold of in-game access. Come playoff time, however, when media attendance increased voluminously, we were more likely to be closer to the ceiling than the court, or in the pressroom, watching on TV. Pregame locker rooms that had once housed some of the most candid mainstream athletes were often empty, as players took refuge in the adjoining trainer's room and succeeding in widening the gulf with an increasingly cynical press.

Many large newspapers, citing deadline-forbidding starting times, cut back on coverage or resigned themselves to using wire copy. Stern had long been a believer in new media, in the power of what people could access on screen, and how technology provided the league a means to filter its own message. He described his product as "twelve hundred episodes of reality programming," but what happened when the reality didn't match the message? What was the risk when passions ran high, where bodies were packed together, and when the liberal consumption of alcohol was routine? *Who Wants to Be a Millionaire* could quickly devolve into the *Jerry Springer Show.*

Like Michelle, Fred, and Stan, Spike Lee had noticed that many of the old courtside regulars, unable to pay what he called "crazy money," now shared their tickets or no longer came at all. He could afford his two seats, but the price was spiraling to the point where he was losing track. "Thirteen," he said when I asked what he paid. When I e-mailed him back to say the Knicks listed Celebrity Row seats as a $1,900 outlay, he responded: "Got my numbers confused: $1900 clams. WHEW!"

Lee occasionally dropped in on other arenas, as when he had business in Miami and watched his old nemesis, the retiring but still sprightly Reggie Miller, and the Pacers beat Shaquille O'Neal and the Heat in early 2005. Their old hostilities a thing of the past, Reggie gave him a hug after the game, but Lee wished more fans could feel the love. "Jim Brown said the players are nothing more than gladiators to a lot of these people and I agree with that," Lee said. "Right after the fight, I heard Charles Barkley say on television that the people coming to these games don't feel good about these young black men making so much money. I agree with that. The money's changed everything." He meant for the fans. As much as the money had altered the players' lifestyles, it had changed the attitude of the fans even more. "Especially," he said, "when the players start playing the fool."

By November 2004, it could be argued that respect for the NBA player had plummeted to a new low, at least for players born in the United States. Even back in the late 1970s, when the sport was harshly critiqued and largely ignored, no one could question the qualitative superiority of the NBA star. But Lee was right. And so were Michelle Musler, Dave Bing, and Fred Klein. The people who had stayed with the sport, front and center, recognized the change in the fan base, the corrosive aftermath of having driven so many loyal patrons away. In their place were many who didn't love the game, couldn't really appreciate the amazing triumph it was for every player who made it to the NBA, as much as they relished the scene. The inflammable conditions created by the alienation between the sport and its fan base hadn't happened overnight but could be traced back more than a decade to a relatively brief period when the globe-trotting NBA became the hottest sports show on earth, beginning in Barcelona in 1992, just weeks after Biasone, the working man's advocate, passed away and his voice of reason was lost, never to be replaced.

3

1992: Barcelona

In November 1991, the images of Magic Johnson announcing from Los Angeles, with fantastic poise and fractured English, that he had "attained" the AIDS virus were beamed all around the world. There wasn't a wired country on earth that wasn't stunned or sobered to learn that the great American basketball star had become one more statistic in an epidemic that stopped at no border and spoke every language.

Magic retired immediately from the Lakers but did not surrender his place on the U.S. Olympic team of NBA professionals that included Michael Jordan, whose fame by the early nineties had spread across oceans and continents. By the summer of 1992, my generation of sportswriters had its transcendent story, a wakeup call on a changing global economy that was about to dramatically change the way all of our sports leagues did business.

For the handful of reporters who accompanied the Dream Team from the Olympic qualifying tournament in Portland, Oregon, to a weeklong training camp in Monte Carlo that preceded the Barcelona Games, it was like being on the road with the basketball Beatles. In Monte Carlo, crowds of French-speaking kids staked out the Loews Monte Carlo for a glimpse of Magic and Michael and, of course, Larry Bird. In an exhibition game against the French national team, three thousand fans chanted

"*Ma-gique . . . Ma-gique,*" and Magic took the opportunity to climb into the royal box and pose for a photo with Prince Albert.

We all knew that basketball, an Olympic sport since 1936 and long played professionally in many countries, had not exactly been a foreign concept in Europe, like baseball or American football. By the late eighties, David Stern forged an alliance with Boris Stankovic, the chief administrator of the international basketball federation called FIBA. They conceived an annual tournament matching pro teams from around the world, and the McDonald's Open became the prelude to NBA players competing in the Olympics, and rerouting the future of the game.

By day, we covered the Dream Team practice, filing our stories before dinner. By night, we strolled the narrow streets, dropped by the old casino, where Jordan—whose predilection for gaming was soon to haunt him in headlines—was usually at the blackjack tables into the wee hours. One night, Bob Ryan (of *The Boston Globe*), Ailene Voisin (then of *The Atlanta Journal-Constitution*), and I drove into Italy and were directed by border security to a small family restaurant in a tranquil hamlet. The pasta and wine tasted of heaven, which is what that summer felt like for us all. The Mediterranean view from the rooftop pool of the Loews Monte Carlo, where the players and their families lounged alongside us, looked nothing like Richfield, Ohio.

The basketball games we covered, at least those the Americans were involved in, were not much to write home about. In Portland at the Olympic qualifying tournament, everyone else had looked so slow, so grounded, so feeble. For NBA players, the games had been dunk-and-pony shows, the opposition more likely to faint in the presence of Jordan, Magic, and company than challenge them at the rim. In one hilarious sequence, a player guarding Magic motioned to a teammate on the bench to snap a photo. The team shots taken after each game had the look of children posing at Christmastime on Santa Claus's lap at the department store. Even Oscar Schmidt, a Brazilian gunner and reigning international star, said he was honored to get his shot repeatedly blocked because, "To play against Magic Johnson and Larry Bird has been my dream."

From the American side of the Atlantic, the Dream Team wasn't much more than colorful pageantry, producing an anti–Miracle on Ice that reinforced the notion of American superiority. The breakup of the Soviet Union and the East German sports machine left no opponents in Barcelona for the United States to take special pride in walloping. Many Americans actually felt squeamish about the millionaire pros descending on the Olympics, still falsely trumpeted as the Mecca of amateurism, forsaking the athletes' village for $900-a-night luxury hotel digs. But dwelling on their celebrity, or the orgasmic marketing orgy for American-based companies and their well-paid pitchmen like Jordan, was Americanizing or missing the point. Stankovic, for one, laughed off the assertion that Stern had manipulated him for the marketing windfall. "Americans are funny that way," he told me several years later during the McDonald's Open in London. "They like to see only what is good for them."

From the parts of the world suddenly getting a view of the West no longer obstructed by the Iron Curtain, the sight of those dashing millionaires, Magic and Michael, was illuminating. The NBA may have envisioned the Dream Team as a once-unfathomable coup for the champions of corporate fidelity, but capitalism was a game millions upon millions suddenly unbound by the shackles of Communism wanted to play. "Those Olympics and that first Dream Team were an international powder keg that created a revolution that affected the far reaches of the earth," said Donny Nelson, one of foremost authorities on the development of the international game. It was his dogged pursuit of a Lithuanian, Sarunas Marciulionis, that brought the Soviet star to the Golden State Warriors, the team coached by Nelson's father, in 1989.

That was also one year after the Soviets beat a team of American collegians coached by John Thompson in the Seoul Olympics in the semifinals, a defeat so embarrassing to the American basketball establishment that it finally called out to its NBA soldiers of fortune. In addition to a Stern orchestration, many people believed it a rash overreaction, but Aleksandr Gomelsky, the Soviet coach, called it "the best thing for basketball." Gomelsky, more than most, understood historical trends of sport and life. Four years after achieving his lifelong dream of Olympic gold, of being tossed in the air like a beach ball by his players, he reached across a table in a hotel lounge in Portland for my notebook and pen. "Let me show you how we beat John Thompson's press," he said.

In the late 1980s, Thompson was at the height of his success as the defensive-minded guru at Georgetown University. His team was stocked with soon-to-be NBA All-Stars: David Robinson, Dan Majerle, Danny Manning, and Mitch Richmond. Early in those Summer Games in Seoul, Gomelsky and his players watched the U.S. collegians press some hopelessly outclassed opponent out of the gymnasium, and one of Gomelsky's assistants whispered to him: "The boys not believe they can win against this press." Gomelsky, five feet, five inches tall, known in world basketball circles as "The Silver Fox," gathered his giants around the next day. "I say, 'Boys, we win against the Atlanta Hawks in Moscow," he said, referring to an earlier exhibition against Ted Turner's NBA team. "I say, 'We win against some of the great American colleges when we tour the States. I believe you win against the press.'"

Every practice session in Seoul, the last Soviet Olympic basketball team worked on breaking Thompson's press and nothing else. By the semifinals, the Soviets had thoroughly incorporated the strategy that Gomelsky so happily scribbled into my notepad, turning it into a geometry text. The result was a barrage of uncontested shots and the second Olympic loss in history for U.S. basketball, both administered by the Soviets, sixteen years apart. For Gomelsky, the symmetry of sixteen was oh so sweet. It was in 1956, or sixteen years before the first gold medal, that he went as an assistant coach to his first Olympics in Melbourne. There, he saw the future of the sport in a tall, skinny black man who anchored the American defense from the rear in a string of numbing blowouts. The center's name was Bill Russell, and by the time he got around to the Soviets, they were grateful to be beaten by a mere 35.

"We cannot compete," Gomelsky said, "but we start to learn." They finally beat the Americans at their own game in 1972, in Munich, in a gold-medal game whose result represents in America the height of international competitive corruption. Not to Gomelsky, though, for whom the infamous replaying of the final three seconds, leading to a game-winning layup, was beside the point. "We could play against them, finally," he said. That was what mattered, nothing else, not even his absence from those Games, his visa revoked because the KGB feared that Gomelsky, a Jew, would defect to the Israeli delegation. The official explanation was that he was replaced for losing a tournament to Yugoslavia the previous year. "Our old system," he said, sheepishly. "Not so good."

With the dismantling of the Berlin Wall in November 1989, the Soviet sports system crumbled, ruble by ruble, brick by brick. By 1992, Gomelsky's boys, as he always called them, were free to pursue contracts worth hundreds of thousands of dollars in Europe and the United States. Marciulionis, a rugged guard, was already a favorite of the Bay Area. Sponsored in part by the Grateful Dead, he and his Lithuanian teammates wound up rocking Barcelona. "We had been doing every speaking engagement we could do to raise money, fifty dollars or seventy-five dollars," Donny Nelson said. "Someone wrote a story in one of the Bay Area papers, and a couple of the Grateful Dead members read it and called to say they wanted to help." Marciulionis had never heard of them, but he went with Nelson to a concert, where he was introduced to the fashions of the tie-dyed nation. By the time they got to Barcelona, the hottest merchandise at the basketball venue was the splashy Lithuania warmup shirt with the skeleton on the front, the Lithuanians' first lesson in Sports Marketing 101.

Though they represented the unbridled capitalism of the

West, Nelson, who signed on as an assistant coach for Lithuania, argued that the Americans were respected least for their money. He remembered the reverence with which the NBA stars were treated, the appreciation for what they meant to the sport. "Everyone knew they were born into an economic lifestyle, or at least achieved one from playing the game," he said. "But anyone who played them, I think money was the last thing they saw. What made them special—and set them apart from all the Dream Teams that followed—was their commitment to teamwork, their dedication, their willingness to do anything to win."

Though it appeared that Dream Team opponents were psyched out, beaten before the first dribble, Gomelsky would argue that the remapping of Eastern Europe was a factor in the Americans' dominance. Gomelsky believed that his 1988 Soviet team, given four additional years and the experience players like Marciulionis gained from playing abroad, would have been no pushover. He had at least one informed supporter, and his name was Chuck Daly.

Retired in Florida, into his seventies, Daly's conversational pace still quickened when he reminisced about those special weeks. He laughingly called himself the greatest coach in history who sat through an entire Olympics without once having to stand up and call timeout. Yet Daly wouldn't dismiss Gomelsky's assertion. Long before NBA players and apologists would begin using international rules as excuses, he studied tapes of international play, saw the potential for trouble with the shorter game (forty minutes as opposed to forty-eight), the wider lane, the ability of European marksmen to wreak havoc from behind the closer 3-point line.

He mentioned having gone to the European championships in Rome the summer before Barcelona to scout the opposition. "I'm sitting there looking at a team with Vlade Divac, Toni Kukoc, Drazen Petrovic, a hell of a team, and I'm thinking, 'I know we're going to have a great team, but this could be the mother of all games.'" He was actually watching Yugoslavia's national team

that night, not the Soviets, who had already dissolved. Soon the
Yugoslavs would meet the same fate, Balkanized and, in the case
of the Serbs, banned from the '92 Games.

Sarunas Marciulionis agreed with Gomelsky and Daly, but
only to a point. "What is compete?" he said. "Minus ten, minus
twenty? Maybe we don't lose by forty." In Barcelona, the United
States obliterated the competition by an average of 43.7 points
per game. Its stiffest competition, its most compelling theater, was
a game-conditions scrimmage in Monte Carlo, when Magic's
squad took a 14–2 lead over Michael's and Magic decided to talk
some trash. Instantly, the gymnasium in the land of princes, high
rollers, and Mercedes-Benz taxis was transformed into a steamy
urban playground. Magic told Jordan that he had better "get into
his show" or the game would be over before he knew it. "I don't
know why I said that," Magic said. Yes, he did. Players at his level
live for such challenges. As Jordan proceeded to demonstrate,
they welcome them, too.

"Michael just kind of took it over for the next couple of minutes," Magic said. Soon the score was close and a riotous battle
ensued, with reporters allowed in just in time to see one of the officials whistle Magic for fouling Jordan on his way to the basket.
"Just like Chicago Stadium," Magic whined, as Jordan stepped to
the free throw line. "Like they picked up Chicago Stadium and
moved it to Monte Carlo." To which Jordan, glancing over his
shoulder and speaking out of the side of his mouth, parried: "Hey,
man, it *is* the nineties."

In the context of the upheaval of those early nineties, the dramatic governmental and ideological changes in Eastern Europe,
the best game of the Barcelona tournament, dripping with politics
and passion, was for the bronze medal. Fate seemed to match
Lithuania with its longtime oppressors, the Russians, or what was
called for those Olympics the Commonwealth of Independent
States. This was a one-time consortium of Russians and players
from the former Soviet satellites whose newly formed nations
hadn't organized their own Olympic teams, or qualified for the

Games. A Lithuania victory set off a celebration on the medal stand every bit as wild as the 1980 U.S. Olympic hockey team's following the Miracle on Ice. The cold-war construct was one thing. These passions resulted from the actual experience of tyranny. "We had the will to prove we were free, able to play under our own flag," Marciulionis said when I reached him in Vilnius in early 2005. He called the medal stand scene "the greatest moment of my life."

Demonstrations of pure nationalism and a more self-serving kind broke out side by side, from one pedestal to another. After the United States won the gold by drubbing the silver medalist and equally jubilant Croatians, Jordan mounted the stand with an American flag draped over his shoulder, championing his shoe company along with his country. He had created a stir earlier in the Games by saying he would not don the stylish sweat Team USA was contractually honored to promote. Jordan, a Nike man, would not wear Reebok. "If the other eleven guys want to wear the suit, that's their choice," said Jordan. "That doesn't mean I have to follow."

As causes go, this wasn't in the league with refusing to step forward for induction into the Army to fight in Vietnam. Jordan was no Muhammad Ali, no beacon of sacrifice as we typically defined it. He was, however, becoming the quintessential agent of celebrity in a world inextricably linked by satellite, the king of corporate sloganism. If Magic suddenly and sadly represented earthly frailty, Air Jordan was considered otherwordly. "You are so good—are you a terrestrial?" he was asked when roughly a thousand journalists pushed their way into the Dream Team's first press conference in Barcelona. Stumbling for an answer, Jordan responded: "No, I live in Chicago."

The Windy City was the center of the basketball universe and America was now the desired destination for millions of young boys with a ball and a dream. By 1992, even Aleksandr Gomelsky had fled far from Moscow and its forbidding winters to sunny San Diego. Before the Barcelona Games, the president of the Russian basketball federation called him, complaining of problems with the Commonwealth team. He begged Gomelsky for help. "How much do you pay?" Gomelsky said. The basketball official, he said, told him, "No money, you are patriot." Gomelsky replied, "No thanks."

For former Communists, the Olympics and sport in general could now be what they were in the West: about nationalism and capitalism, or whichever at the moment was the more expedient objective. But some athletes had more motivation than others in how to blend these extremely divergent concepts. When Marciulionis quit the NBA in 1997, he returned home and invested a huge chunk of the great fortune he'd amassed, by Lithuanian standards, in a professional league. Then he started a basketball academy in Vilnius and built a hotel next door to support it. "His agent told him he was crazy," Nelson said. Marciulionis, the ultimate player-patriot, wasn't listening. His money was put to prideful use, helping to develop the next generation of Lithuanian players, setting a glowing example of how to give back. By comparison, the American role model during the nineties was Jordan, conscientious objector for corporate America.

However history would come to view this exceedingly apolitical man, there was no denying that much of what set Jordan apart were lessons learned in the era led by Magic and Bird. Jordan's grasp of the game's fundamentals, his abiding commitment to competition, was a testament to the eighties, to three years spent with Dean Smith at North Carolina, where he wasn't handed the keys to the program, or given license to shoot whenever he felt the urge. In the eighties and early nineties, the best NBA decade-plus, players mixed the advanced athleticism of the late twentieth century with a firm grasp of throwback fundamentals from the days of Russell and Robertson. In pre-expansion days, eighties championship teams—the Celtics, the Lakers, the 76ers, and, later, Daly's Pistons—featured All-Stars up and down the lineup. In 1985, you could run a scan of NBA rosters and come up with two dozen future Hall of Famers. Counting contemporary futures such as LeBron James and Dwyane Wade, you would be hard-pressed to reach fifteen in today's league. More teams. Fewer legends.

"You had the two best teams, Boston and L.A, with so many great players, Hall of Fame frontlines, and of course Magic and Bird," Daly said. His own two-time champion Detroit Pistons, headlined by Isiah Thomas and Joe Dumars, had quality players at every position and off the bench. "The Dream Team was really a celebration of those years," Daly said. "And the best thing about those guys was how seriously they were in wanting to protect the mystique they had. Coach K [Duke coach Mike Krzyzewski, an Olympic assistant to Daly] always talked about that, but they already knew and you knew it just by being around them."

Daly could still conjure up the compelling imagery of the team's bus ride from the hotel in Portland before the first qualifying tournament game. "So quiet it felt like game seven," Daly said. He couldn't recall the opponent anymore (Cuba) or the size of the victory (79 points). It didn't matter. The tension said more about what those players expected of themselves. "They make better cars elsewhere and better audiovisual equipment," Charles Barkley said after that game. "Cuba's got cigars. We've got basketball."

After a game or two, it was obvious that only a biblical act could beat the Dream Team but, as Daly said, "The beauty about them was they took nothing for granted." Those five words—they took nothing for granted—bared the elemental difference between the 1980s NBA and the epochs to follow. Over the years, it has become axiomatic to say that the NBA renaissance began the minute Magic and Bird arrived in the fall of 1979, fresh off their showdown in the NCAA championship game, won by Magic's Michigan State team over Bird and Indiana State. That was not the case, far from it. While the fan bases quickly revved up in Boston and Los Angeles, while the media quickly seized on the racial subtext of the charismatic black man orchestrating Showtime in Hollywood against the taciturn white man invigorating blue-collar Boston, the NBA as a national entity still lagged far behind the popularity of baseball and football.

Magic's legendary rookie performance—the achievement he told me that he ranks above all others—went virtually unwatched, by later Nielsen standards. On May 16, 1980, the Friday night Magic dropped 42 points on the 76ers in Philadelphia while subbing at center for the injured Kareem Abdul-Jabbar to clinch his first of five championships, I filed my story for the Saturday *New York Post* and drove the ninety miles back to my apartment in Brooklyn Heights, flipped on CBS, and watched the fourth quarter all over again. In the all-important New York City market, the Finals clincher was not important enough to preempt a rerun of *Dallas,* and was shown instead on delayed tape.

Players such as Magic and Bird, and the holdover seventies stars like Julius Erving and Kareem Abdul-Jabbar knew exactly where they were in the pro sports pecking order. They knew what America's perceptions of them were, fair or not, and they listened when their union director, Larry Fleisher, detailed the dire financial straits several franchises were in. They compromised with the owners, agreeing in 1983 to a team salary structure, or cap. And as the league moved into the mid-1980s, as Stern became commissioner and began to work his promotional wizardry, the stars embraced his eye-catching gimmickry. When a slam-dunk contest was instituted at All-Star Weekend, the preeminent fliers like Jordan and Dominique Wilkins, could be counted on to participate. When they added a three-point shooting competition, Bird took it as an insult that anyone believed he could lose.

Through the years, Bird was made into a lot of things by people who hailed him as the torch carrier for his race in a sport increasingly dominated by blacks. He was hailed as white players too often were—scrappier and smarter, the hardest worker. In a sport where athleticism was myopically defined by one's end-to-end speed and vertical leap, Bird's physical assets—his soft hands, amazing peripheral vision, and ambidexterity—were routinely underplayed. Though he was born for blue-collar Boston, the sharpshooter in baggy jeans and flannel shirt headlining an arena known for dressing down, Bird was always his own, independent man. But while his NBA years will forever be known as the Bird-Magic era, the annals of the sport don't lie. Magic won five NBA titles to Bird's three. Counting the NCAA final, Magic beat Bird three of four in championship showdowns. For fans black and white, Magic made basketball matter in a way it never had before. He was a revolutionary player, a six-nine point guard who embodied the game at its multitasking best, who could simultaneously please with individual panache but always within the context of the team.

The true beauty of Magic was not how fast he ran, how high he jumped, how much he assisted or scored. It was how well and quickly he thought, as when he made what was arguably his most brilliant pass of all, a slow bouncer to no one that drained the final seconds of a Western Conference final against Portland in 1991. "It wasn't just on the court," said Josh Rosenfeld, a former Lakers' public relations director. "When we'd hold our preseason scrimmage, we'd have an autograph session and Earvin would tell all the players where to sit, just to make sure none of the fringe guys would wind up off by themselves. When we'd have a meeting before his charity game every summer, he'd ask: 'What are we doing for public relations, for marketing, for ticket sales?' You'd better have an answer, too." To those who knew Earvin the way the rest of us knew Magic, it was no surprise that he eventually would launch a business career and be extolled in the country's largest media outlets for bringing major corporations to inner cities. You could say he became the American Marciulionis.

Basketball historians and purists have argued that Oscar Robertson, for one, was Magic long before Magic was, and with a jump shot to boot. But Magic was blessed to land with a talent-laden team, born with a personality and in a time that enabled him to become the most telegenic athlete America had seen. Flashing down the court with his trademark high dribble, his eyes seeing all, he had the style and smile to launch a thousand new networks. He was irresistibly hip and fun, unthreatening, and exceedingly appealing to white America. Basketball's Cosby helped change the demographic rules, made people want to be part of *his* extended family. Magic was usually happy to oblige them.

He was a beloved figure, and by the summer of '92 had generated tremendous respect for the courage he showed by putting himself on the world's grand sports stage as the new face of HIV. "I was afraid that our guys, especially Magic, would overshadow the other athletes," Daly said. The reality was something quite different. At the opening ceremonies, the fencers and the kayakers and even the world-renowned track stars flocked to Magic's side, with their cameras and VCRs. At the basketball arena, I stumbled upon a more spontaneous display of Magic's uncommon ability to make forever friends and fans.

The usual postgame mob scene in the bowels of the Palau d'Esports in the suburb of Badalona—a mixture of excited back-slappers and exasperated journalists—was winding down. I was finished with my interviewing, when I noticed a very tall, thin white man with a media pass dangling from his neck approach Magic. "Earvin, it's good to see you," the man said, holding out his hand. Magic looked up, and without pause, flashed his famous smile. "Sten, how you doing?" The name rolled off his tongue as if they had met the previous week for lunch. They hugged and talked for a few minutes. Intrigued, I followed Sten down the corridor and back toward the pressroom. "I saw you with Magic back there," I said. "Are you an old friend?"

Sten Feldreich, a Swede who was covering the Olympics for a magazine back home in Stockholm, proceeded to tell me about the year he had spent playing basketball at Michigan State, as a six-foot-eleven twenty-two-year-old import from the Swedish national team. Jud Heathcote, the Michigan State coach, had told him: "If you come with us, you can have a scholarship and be seven feet." Feldreich went to East Lansing, where he played with the freshman sensation, Earvin Johnson. They were not best friends, he said, but there were Sunday afternoons when Johnson would see him lounging around the dorm, no family to visit, and would invite him to his parents' home in nearby Lansing. They would sit around sipping Magic's beverage of choice, Hawaiian Punch, and watch the NBA game of the week.

Homesick, Feldreich left Michigan before the NCAA championship run that was engineered by Magic the following season, never to see Johnson until that day in Barcelona. Fourteen years' worth of hands being thrust at him, of people wanting an interview or an autograph, of associations and acquaintances, real and imagined, and Johnson, in a heartbeat, knew the face, even if he read the name from the credential. "Most people would probably not remember," Feldreich said. "Actually, I would have been surprised and a little disappointed if he hadn't. It wouldn't be like Earvin."

Nor would it have been like Magic to let himself be cast aside as a celebrity leper after announcing he was carrying the virus, twenty-four hours after hearing the news himself. The reservoir of goodwill he had generated over the years had even helped him live down the indelicate revelations regarding his sexual appetite and habits. His presence at the Olympics softened the public relations blows for Jordan in the medal-suit flap, for the typically impolitic Charles Barkley, who got into the Olympic spirit by elbowing a skinny economics student from war-torn Angola, a professed Barkley fan.

Putting those Olympics in their proper context was no difficult chore for those of us who covered the Bird-Magic years, who watched Bird weave his own magic in Boston and Magic emulate the begoggled Kareem with a game-winning sky hook in the Finals, and who still snap to attention when a Lakers-Celtics classic shows up on ESPN. We knew an extraordinary run was ending. Though Bird didn't announce his retirement until he returned to Boston, he was finished, his body breaking down, his aching back making him a marginal Olympic presence. No one cheered louder than Magic when Bird, on a rare pain-free day, poured in 19 points in twenty minutes in a rout of Germany. Magic jumped off the bench just like a Southie in Boston Garden when Bird, experiencing an amnesiac moment, dove on the floor for a loose ball. They had developed a kinship second to none in the history of competing NBA players, but Bird couldn't play and Magic, HIV notwithstanding, still could. In the season before he'd quit, Magic averaged 19 points, 12.5 assists, and 7 rebounds, and led the Lakers into the Finals. For all the calls for him to be an advocate for the HIV-infected, he believed he could best lead by example. In September, he surprised none of us by ending his retirement and rejoining the Lakers.

As training camps for the 1992–93 season began, as Barcelona's glow began to fade, there was much to write about for NBA reporters, compelling change in the hierarchy of stars. Jordan was now defending champion, master of the NBA universe. Bird was gone. Magic was back. And as far as we could tell, or based on the Olympic love-in, he was returning to a brass section of approval and acclaim. But that was before I ran into Karl Malone, who slam-dunked the notion that NBA players were sufficiently informed on the risks of banging bodies with a player carrying the AIDS virus, or sanguine about his comeback. "The Dream Team was a concept everybody loved," Malone said. "But now we're back to reality. Just because he came back doesn't mean nothing to me. I'm no fan, no cheerleader."

It was a Tuesday evening, and I'd wandered from *The New York Times* office on West Forty-third Street down to Madison Square Garden just below Thirty-fourth, in search of material for a welcome-back Magic feature I was preparing. Sitting by himself, half undressed in the small visitors' dressing room a couple of hours before a preseason game, Malone recognized me from our many summer days on the road. We made small talk for a few minutes, and then I changed the subject to Magic's comeback and the positive publicity it was generating for the sport. Malone, who always makes strong eye contact in interviews, let me finish my little dissertation and then pointed to a small, pinkish hole on his thigh that was developing an outer crust. "Look at this, scabs and cuts all over me," he said. "I get these every night, every game. They can't tell you that you're not at risk, and you can't tell me there's one guy in the NBA who hasn't thought about it."

Malone went on to say he was certain his competitive instincts would take over in the heat of competition and he would not avoid contact with Magic. But he couldn't vouch for his team-mates; he worried about the competition being tainted. "That concerns me," he said, "because I'm only here to win." Malone, from the Louisiana backwoods, was far from the cookie-cutter pro athlete. A mountain of a man whose pastime was driving rigs around the west, he was often outspoken, with opinions often far from the center. So rather than rush his comments into print and hang Malone out to dry as a lone dissenter, I decided to report out the story, find out how widespread the fear of playing against Magic really was.

The league had already implemented several precautionary measures, forcing any player cut to immediately leave the floor. In addition, the Players Association developed a health-education program in conjunction with a physician at Johns Hopkins University. A brochure circulated to every player stated that HIV "is not spread through contact during sports activities." The odds of contracting the virus from Magic were no doubt smaller than a team plane going down, but clinical assurances apparently weren't enough. Open family dialogue was needed, but the commissioner's office was strangely silent. "We spent weeks closeted around here," Stern recalled. "How do we respond to this? What do we do? Who the hell knows?"

What many players knew, as I soon discovered, was what their wives and girlfriends were warning them of. As Malone had said, fear was widespread, of the disease and of speaking out against Magic. Gerald Wilkins, a Cleveland guard, actually lowered his voice to a whisper on the telephone when he said, "Everybody's talking about it. Some people are scared." That weekend, the Lakers played a preseason game against Cleveland

and Magic sustained a small cut. A wire photo showed him being treated on the bench by the trainer, Gary Vitti, who was not wearing gloves. The next day, Sunday, my *Times* story ran, leading with Malone's quotes but including the comments of several other players and team officials, some requesting anonymity, who were skeptical or afraid. Much to my relief, Malone did not back away from the quotes, as many less-forthright athletes would have done. Magic quit, again, saying he'd detected fear in the eyes of some Cavaliers.

Professionally, my story was a coup, widely cited in the media frenzy that followed. Personally, it pained me to write it. There wasn't an athlete I'd derived more pleasure in watching and writing about than Magic Johnson. There wasn't a player or person I believed more responsible for the sport's surge of popularity. I also believed that Malone, predictably vilified for his political incorrectness, was not to blame. At least he was honest, unafraid to create a dialogue that wasn't a whisper. But it was too late. The lack of public discourse led to an unenlightened denouement. As a result, everyone lost.

Magic joined Bird on the sideline, attending Bird's retired jersey ceremony, which was such a happening in Boston that it was held at the Garden on a night the Celtics weren't even playing. Magic's jersey was already hanging in the rafters of the Great Western Forum, Bird ignoring doctors' advice against a cross-country flight with his bad back to make the celebration. This time, during a two-hour, twenty-five-minute, Bob Costas–emceed production, the old rivals exchanged Olympic diamond commemorative rings, hugged tight, and promised to accompany each other upon their guaranteed Hall of Fame inductions.

Happening to glance down press row at the moment the old foes and friends embraced, I saw something I'd never seen and haven't seen since—sinfully cynical sportswriters with tears in their eyes. Who could imagine Boston Garden, that lovable old dump, without Larry Bird? Who even wanted to consider where Magic would be by the time of his Hall of Fame election?

In Monte Carlo, sitting around with Magic one afternoon, he

had told a few of the writers that his doctor had advised him to eat well, continue to exercise, and, above all, maintain a positive attitude. "Being positive is what I'm all about," he said, with a trademark smile and a gleam in his eye that suggested he had been handed a cure, not a death sentence. When he left, the writers looked at each other squeamishly, wondering how long before we would be haunted by those words. Yet five years after his initial retirement, Magic was not only breathing, he was once again playing, looking healthy as an ox and, given the advances in medication, showing what doctors called undetectable levels of HIV in his blood.

Never comfortable with how he'd allowed himself to be exiled by fear in the fall of '92, he returned to a young and relatively marginal Lakers team at age thirty-seven. As comebacks go, it was brief, lasting thirty-two games, mostly unhappy, and lent credence to the belief that the perfect Hollywood ending for Magic would have been on that medal stand in Barcelona, alongside Larry Bird. Jordan had been right that day in Monte Carlo. The feel-good eighties were over. It was, indeed, the nineties. Fueled in part by Barcelona, the years ahead would produce for the NBA windfalls of dollars, with one serious tradeoff: The sport we knew and loved was about to make much less sense.

4

1993: The Double-Edged Legacy of Michael Jordan

MICHAEL JORDAN'S SIX-TIME TITLE RUN with the Chicago Bulls lasted through 1998, but the symbolic climax of basketball's golden era, the end of the extended eighties, came on a steamy Sunday night, June 20, 1993, at Phoenix's America West Arena. Jordan and the Bulls were one win away from a third straight championship, the prized three-peat, or a defeat away from a seventh game, on the road, against a Suns team that had won a league-best sixty-two regular-season games. Two-time champions and the game's greatest player notwithstanding, many basketball people believed going into the series that the Suns were the better team, that it was Charles Barkley's time to breathe the rarified air of NBA reverence, as the franchise player on a championship team.

The Bulls, in fact, weren't even the first playoff seed in the Eastern Conference that season. They won three fewer games than Pat Riley's thuggish Knicks, who believed they were finally locked and loaded for their first championship since 1973, with their star-crossed center, Patrick Ewing, taking aim at Jordan, his longtime nemesis. With home-court advantage in the conference finals, the Knicks took the first game at Madison Square Garden. But at halftime of game two—another Knicks' victory, punctuated by a rousing, left-handed dunk in the face of Jordan by the rambunctious John Starks—Dave Anderson wandered over to where I was furiously typing on my laptop, behind the basket closest to the visitors' bench. Anderson, the *Times*'s venerable columnist, mentioned that the fans behind the basket near where he was sitting—directly across from me, in the vicinity of Fred Klein and Stan Asofsky—had been heckling Jordan throughout the game. Something about gambling in Atlantic City.

"Let me see what I can find out," I told him, and made a beeline for Fred and Stan, who identified a man sitting several rows behind them as the source of the scoop. This fan, believing he was acting in the Knicks' best interests, was thrilled to share what he'd seen: Jordan in the baccarat pit in Bally's Grand casino, into the early morning hours. Armed with this information, Anderson, well connected in Atlantic City boxing circles, set out the next day to confirm the story. A Bally's source told him that Jordan had appeared at the hotel at seven after five in the afternoon and was seen as late as two thirty in the morning. Factoring in the two-hour ride back to midtown Manhattan, even giving Jordan the benefit of the doubt, he couldn't have been back to the hotel and in bed until the vicinity of four thirty or five.

As the series returned to Chicago, the *Times* appeared with Anderson's column raising questions about Jordan's decision to stay out that late: He was thirty years old; he had been playing virtually nonstop for two years after the '92 title run, followed by the Dream Team adventure and the nearly ten-month 1992–93 season; he had seemed to tire in the fourth quarter of game one. Didn't Superman need an occasional rest? As Anderson pointed out, there was also the overriding issue of Jordan's continued and troublesome associations with gambling: Checks totaling $108,000 and another for $57,000 that were signed by Jordan or drawn on an account used by his agents had surfaced in criminal investigations the previous year. Jordan had explained the gambling away as something he enjoyed in his leisure time. Here, however, was the first indication that it was affecting his ability to prioritize, that his innocent little pastime was out of control. What was going on with basketball's preeminent star?

Jordan's answer was to shut down communication with the media for the remainder of the series, which the NBA, as usual, was helpless to do much about, except to fine him what amounted to a child's allowance. As usual with Jordan, the controversy was forgotten as soon as he tightened his Nike laces and put on his game face. He proceeded to lead the Bulls to victories in the next four games, leaving the Knicks, Fred, Stan, Spike, and, of course, Michelle Musler still without a championship and cursing the messengers, Anderson and the *Times,* for apparently refocusing Jordan on the task at hand. And thus did the Bulls, leading the Finals 3–2, return to America West Arena, where they engaged Barkley and the Suns in a fierce game six struggle.

Beginning the fourth quarter with an 8-point lead, the Bulls seemed poised to close out the series but suddenly went cold. Six minutes elapsed without Chicago scoring a point. With 14.1 seconds left, the Suns led 98–96. The Bulls, in possession of the ball, had scored 9 points in the quarter, on their way to the lowest-scoring quarter in a Finals game since the adoption of Danny Biasone's 24-second shot clock. Jordan had scored them all.

In the Bulls' huddle during the timeout, Phil Jackson asked his players if they wanted to go for broke, shoot a 3-pointer. Even with the safety net of game seven, he was being facetious. When Jackson became the Bulls' coach in 1989, he was praised for diversifying the Jordan-ruled Bulls' attack with the triangle offense, a scheme predicated on balancing the floor to create ball movement and require all five players to participate in the flow. Naturally, it didn't hurt that Jackson also had Jordan, the mad scientist of one-on-one, to inevitably bail him out when egalitarianism failed to produce a quality shot and the 24-second clock was winding down. With that in mind, with only 14.1 seconds with which to work, there wasn't a person in the arena or in a massive international television audience (one year after Barcelona, there were satellite feeds to 109 countries) that didn't expect the ball to be in Jordan's hands, come hell or high water.

But, as Jordan dribbled out of the backcourt, Scottie Pippen flashed to the top of the key and Jordan whipped him the ball. Pippen was supposed to catch the pass, return the ball to Jordan flaring out on the wing. Even on Jordan's team there was some creative license. When Barkley foolishly gambled, reaching for the steal, stumbling by Pippen like a drunk exiting a bar, Pippen whirled and with his gangly, antelope stride, drove into the lane. The unplanned penetration meant that the Suns' Mark West, whose defensive assignment was Horace Grant, had to leave his man to prevent Pippen from reaching the rim. Drawing the help defense, Pippen shoveled a pass to Grant, to the left of the basket, for what might have been a game-tying dunk, had Grant been thinking dunk. But shooting even the highest of percentage shots was the last thing on Grant's mind, after he'd scored a combined 2 points in games five and six and after botching a sure slam minutes earlier by fumbling a perfect setup by Jordan.

Out front, left of the key, John Paxson had stationed himself right behind the 3-point line, "in case something happened." Paxson, a shooter in career sunset, had had an eight-year run with the Bulls, predating Jackson, Pippen, and Grant. Paxson was a rare player who had earned Jordan's trust in the days when Jordan, surrounded by a motley cast, was considered by basketball purists to be a breathtaking scoring machine but more of a sideshow to Magic and Larry's blueprints for triumph. Out on the wing, Paxson found himself alone when Danny Ainge, seeing the play develop near the basket, drifted away. Handling the ball as if it were radioactive, Grant found Paxson, who squared up on rickety knees and released this historic shot while telling himself, "Catch and shoot, like I've done thousands of times."

As the ball settled into the net, as America West Arena went mute, Clifton Brown, the other *Times* reporter sitting next to me in the auxiliary press section halfway to the sky, grabbed my left arm and nearly jumped out of his seat. We looked at each other and broke into knowing smiles.

Sportswriters are forever reminded how lucky we are to be at games fans pay hundreds of dollars to attend, but the NBA play-offs are long, grueling, and life-disrupting, two months of crazy city-hopping, stressful late-night story-filing. Spring can be an annual rumor, along with your child's t-ball season and school family picnic. Had the Bulls lost that sixth game, there would have been another interminable three-day wait for game seven on Wednesday night, followed by a long flight home on the following day. Cliff had his reasons to want to get the series over with. I had mine. Back in Brooklyn Heights, my wife was eight months pregnant with our second child, looking after the three-year-old, and trying to keep her wits about her as we prepared to close on the sale of our coop and move to Montclair, New Jersey—all on Friday morning. Thanks to Paxson, I was home with four days to spare. In our own way, Beth and I were as grateful as the Bulls were.

Professionally speaking, those of us who had logged the miles across the eighties and into the nineties also had to applaud another proud NBA moment, the improvisational grandeur of those decisive seconds. In the haste of making deadline, I began my column for the next morning's paper by writing: "Let that play be shown again and again, and its executors linked in partnership, in making the Chicago Bulls' case for greatness. Score it for the firm of Jordan, Pippen, Grant and Paxson." But when I returned to my hotel room and watched the replay on ESPN, I felt the familiar dread of seeing what I'd just described and realizing that I had missed a small but essential point that would have strengthened my case. When the Bulls had put the ball into play from the back-court, Jordan had passed it to B. J. Armstrong, who gave it right back. Armstrong's role was hardly prominent but officially the ball had touched the hands of all five Bulls. Paxson himself had no idea until he watched a replay much later. That sequence, he said, "was what basketball—what teamwork and success—are all about."

Not surprisingly, in Chicago, the years were kind to Paxson. He, not Jackson or Jordan or Pippen, wound up replacing Jerry Krause as the Bulls' general manager, and succeeded in returning them to the playoffs in 2004–05 for the first time since Jordan left before the lockout-shortened 1998–99 season. Looking all the way back to 1993, Paxson acknowledged that he, as much as Jordan, was the toast of the town in the months following his shot. Offers for speaking engagements poured in, and Paxson relished the opportunity to preach teamwork to corporate cowboys, to school kids, to break the play down to its fundamental bones. "The whole sequence was perfect for what I wanted to say," he said, and especially a few words on behalf of Pippen. "Scottie could've easily just thrown it back to Michael and let him bail us out."

Had Pippen done so, that would no doubt have played into the hands of the mythmakers, who always preferred to cast Jordan as a virtual miracle worker. Magic had lucked into Kareem Abdul-Jabbar and other quality players as a Lakers rookie. By his second season, Bird was playing on a Hall of Fame frontline that included Robert Parish and Kevin McHale. As many an NBA superstar could attest, a playoff legacy often depended as much on serendipity as one's skills set. As the years passed, it became increasingly difficult to stockpile talent as the Lakers and Celtics had, given expansion (to thirty teams by 2004–05) and the constraints of the salary cap.

In Chicago and elsewhere, people often seemed to forget that Jordan did not win a championship until his seventh NBA season, or until Pippen had his back. Jordan usually played along with his own deification, referring to his teammates as his "supporting cast." The day before Paxson's shot, even Jackson, who should have known better, called Jordan's mates his "entourage of players." The media had its own unflattering appellation: Jordanaires. In retrospect, I am not proud of the number of times I resorted to it myself, shortchanging the others, a colorful, personable bunch in their fire-engine-red road unis, featuring Pippen's elasticity and the begoggled Grant's cerebral frontline play, and, later on, the robo rebounding of Dennis Rodman.

In my home, at least, Jordan wasn't the only inimitable Bull. While interviewing Grant after a Bulls' practice at their facility in suburban Chicago during one of their playoff runs, I pulled out a snapshot of a three-and-one-half-year-old boy, bouncing a toy ball on a living room floor, wearing a Bulls' T-shirt and shorts, and red sunglasses with the lens cut out. Grant howled, took the photo from me, and scribbled on the back: "To Alex, Horace Grant, # 54." Twelve years later, the photo remained on my son's bedroom shelf, above his computer.

There was never any argument about Jordan being the best player, the NBA's most spectacular and relentless scorer, and, arguably, the most ruthlessly fierce competitor ever. While basketball's leading men had always helped themselves to more of the promotional pie, never in the history of the sport had a championship team been so thoroughly cast in one man's image. Never had there been a vehicle like the Nike marketing machine to glorify the exploits of a single player. By the time the Bulls won their first title in 1991, Jordan was so big he blew off the Bulls' White House photo op with the president, George H. W. Bush, who, it turned out, could have used the splash for his failed 1992 reelection campaign. Considering much of the Bulls' success was attributable to their hyperactive team defense, the portrayal of his teammates as Santa's little helpers became dramatically overplayed and annoyingly simplistic and unfair. And then, on the eve of training camp in 1993, the Jordanaires were presented with an opportunity to prove their own worth.

Claiming to be bitter over the gambling headlines, haunted by the grisly murder of his father, James, on a dark North Carolina roadside weeks after the third championship, Jordan announced he was leaving the sport. Though it was speculated—never proven—that he had made a secret arrangement with Stern to take a leave of absence in lieu of a gambling suspension, Jordan claimed that he had accomplished what he'd set out to do, winning three straight championships, one-upping Magic, and preferred to stay home with his family. Then Mr. Domesticity proceeded to pack up for Birmingham, Alabama, to fail at breaking balls for a White Sox farm team in a Just Do It campaign to become a baseball player. In two years, the NBA had seen off its three ranking Barcelona legends and now its showcase team would be lucky to stand up to a gust of Chicago's winter wind.

"We still had our core group," said Bill Cartwright, the center on the first three championship teams. "We just didn't have our superstar." Historically, in the NBA, this had been a recipe for mediocrity, or worse. In the season following Bill Russell's retirement, the Celtics went from league champion to thirty-four-win doormats. When Magic abruptly quit in 1991, the Lakers went from league finalist to forty-three-win first-round playoff losers. When Bird departed the Boston Garden stage, the Celtics managed to win forty-eight games, but they had already infused their lineup with young talent, as Bird's body broke down over a period of time. When the Lakers traded Shaquille O'Neal in 2004 and retooled their three-time championship team around Kobe Bryant, they nosedived right out of the playoffs.

On opening night at Chicago Stadium, the Bulls received their championship rings to thunderous roars that grew to a crescendo for Jordan. Dressed immaculately, he put his hand in for one last team huddle, one irresistible photo op, then took a seat with his family in the stands for the player introductions. Chicago Stadium's player intros were the league standard, a high-tech, ear-splitting, goose-bump-inducing treat, for as long as they finished with the spotlight finding number twenty-three in the Bulls' home whites with red trim. On that night, the choreographers must have been stuck in downtown traffic; when it was time for the introduction of the fifth and final Bull, out trotted the journeyman defensive specialist, Pete Myers. Out of the arena went the air of excitement, followed by thousands of sobered fans, long before the conclusion of a blowout loss to Miami.

Along the way to oblivion, the strangest thing happened. The Bulls began stringing together victories, developing an identity without Jordan and around Pippen. By the time I caught up with them again, in Boston on the way into Madison Square Garden for a late November game against the Knicks, they didn't look much like an entourage. They didn't sound like one either. "With all due respect to Michael, we didn't win three championships just because of one guy," B. J. Armstrong had the audacity to say. He was right, though. The Jordanless Bulls of 1993–94 went on to win fifty-five regular-season games, or two fewer than they'd won with Jordan the previous year. It was a shocking development considering they had lost the 32.6 points per game Jordan had averaged the season before and that their only significant addition was Toni Kukoc, an NBA rookie. Jerry Krause, the general manager, years later told me that that season was "the most fun we ever had"—a dubious claim for a six-time champion franchise but more understandable given how little credit was left over after Jordan was given, and accepted, his share.

Of all contributing Bulls' employees, Jordan had the least use for Krause, who joined the team's front office after Jordan was drafted. Krause obtained Pippen in a brilliant draft-day trade with Seattle and acquired every other piece to the Bulls' championship teams, including Phil Jackson. He was not an easy man to get along with by any means, but Jordan refused to give him his due, cut him some slack. He ridiculed Krause for many things, including his portly, decidedly nonathletic physique. The more Jordan refused to acknowledge Krause's role in the building of the Bulls, the more powerful was his message, unintentional or not, that one man and one man only was responsible for their success.

This debate always tilted in Jordan's favor, especially in Chicago, where popular columnists like Bob Greene curried favor with him as if he were the pope. Middle-aged sportswriters, mostly white, could relate to Jordan, who didn't wear tattoos, wasn't into rap, hacked away just like them on the golf course, and even relished a good cigar. He played the part of the good family man and was generally applauded for it, even though writers at least had to suspect otherwise. But the 1993–94 Bulls' regular season should at least have raised some serious questions about the standard characterization of Jordan and the Bulls. Phil Jackson won six titles as the Bulls' coach and three more in Los Angeles, but 1993–94 was the best coaching he's ever done, and the truest measure of Pippen's worth as the Bulls' number-two star. "Let me tell you what the best thing Scottie did all that season," John Paxson said. "He didn't try to be Michael, not for one game, and you know the pressure on him to do that in Chicago was unbelievable. Scottie was just Scottie. He didn't try to score forty points because that's not him. He played his all-around game. He got other players involved, and that's the reason that team did as well as it did."

Eye-opening as those fifty-five wins should have been, basketball superstars inevitably make their money, create their legacies, in the playoffs. In the spring of '94, Pippen and the Bulls had their chance to bust Jordan's ghost, drawing the Knicks in a second-round rematch and finding themselves in another two-game hole. Returning home for game three, the Bulls built a huge fourth-quarter lead, but the Knicks rallied furiously to tie the game with 1.8 seconds left. During a timeout, Jackson set up the play, calling for Pippen to inbound the ball and Kukoc to take the shot from the top of the key. "The same play we always ran for Michael," Cartwright said.

The strategy made sense because Pippen, great multitasker that he was, was far from the classic catch-and-shoot jump shooter. He knew that, but in the heat of the moment, in the glare of the playoffs, he was vanquished by his own pride. Pippen was aghast that a rookie with no championship rings, a Croat who didn't know the Kennedy Expressway from the Fitzgerald, was being given the last shot instead of him. He blew a gasket, sat down on the bench, ignoring Jackson's calls and Cartwright's pleas. "The interesting thing is that had Phil waited another five seconds to break the huddle, I think I could have got Scottie back in there," Cartwright told me. "But Phil, being who he is, said, screw it, I'll go without him."

Myers made the pass. Kukoc hit the shot. In the locker room, Jackson, no control freak, said nothing. In a defining display of coaching genius, he preferred to let the players deal with Pippen and his betrayal. Cartwright, the old pro, angrily confronted Pippen, with tears in his eyes. "How could you, Scottie?" he asked. Pippen apologized and the reenergized Bulls proceeded to even the series and return to New York for a fifth game that was not only pivotal for the series but had a seismic effect, I came to believe, on the future of the sport.

Just as they'd done the previous spring, the Bulls rattled the Knicks late in the game, took a 1 point lead in the dying seconds and clamped down for a last defensive stand. That's when the night turned complicated and cruel, when a ref named Hue Hollins made a fateful call on Pippen for the faintest of fouls, putting Hubert Davis on the free throw line with 2.1 seconds left. Coming from inside the lane, extending his long arms as Davis squared up for a desperation shot with one foot on the 3-point line, Pippen made Davis rush his shot, misfire, but with the flick of a wrist, the toot of a whistle, a script that surely would have demythologized Michael was shredded into a thousand pieces of woulda-coulda scrap.

Jackson was beside himself, raging at Hollins backstage, and years later told me that the 87–86 loss was the most gut wrenching of his career. "I've seen a lot of things in the NBA, but I've never seen anything happen at the end of the game like that," he said. The call provoked one of those neverending basketball conundrums: Who deserved what, and when? Would Jordan or any other certified NBA superstar have been hit with a foul for such incidental contact, for getting a small piece of Davis's hand well after the ball had left it? Pippen's many critics—their ranks swelled following the 1.8 second sit-down at the end of game two—argued that the call was a poetic form of outlaw justice. He had acted like a child, not a superstar, not a leader, and payback was a bitch.

Cartwright, serving as an assistant coach for the New Jersey Nets during the 2004–05 season, shook his head ruefully when I reopened this old wound after a workout at the team's practice facility in a sterile north Jersey industrial park complex. "Let me tell you something," he said. "When that kind of stuff happens, you never forget. And that just cannot happen—a referee's call deciding a game of that magnitude, unless it's a blatant foul. The officials will argue that the calls are the same, even though everyone knows that's not how it is and not how it should be. That call against Pip was not only a questionable foul. It was a late call. Holy shit, the fucking ball came off the back of the rim and then he blows his whistle?"

I had known Cartwright from the time when we were both rookies, me for the *New York Post* and him for the Knicks. This University of San Francisco grad was as West Coast as they come, a soft-spoken giant, not a man disposed to profanity. His voice had been reduced by throat surgery to a scratchy whisper, but now he came across loud and clear. He and everyone else on that Bulls' team would never forget or forgive Hue Hollins. They would take to their graves the memory of being so excruciatingly close to command of that series, to moving on to the conference finals, to chugging along to the next round on the way to making history as the Supporting Cast That Could.

Hubert Davis made his free throws. The Bulls fought to the bitter end before losing in game seven. Had Hue Hollins not called the game five foul, had he followed the unwritten protocol that Pippen had not obstructed Davis's shot, the Bulls would very likely have gone on to play the Indiana Pacers in the conference finals. They had beaten the Pacers four of five games during the regular season. They had split two games with the Western Conference champion Houston Rockets. Conspiracy theories abounded, as usual. It was said the league preferred the New York market moving on, instead of the Jordanless Bulls. As usual, the theories were absurd. The Bulls making the finals would have been compelling theater, another ratings bonanza. Jordan's virtual presence would have been guaranteed by his absence. And if the Bulls had managed to win without him, how could he have been deified as the greatest player of all time? How could he have returned, as the most leveraged commodity in the history of American team sports? Hollins's call changed the texture of the decade—and not for the better, given the standard of franchise-player power-wielding Jordan would set—and may well have deprived the NBA its greatest team-first coup in the history of the sport.

Instead, the Knicks slogged their way past the Pacers but lost in the Finals to Hakeem Olajuwon and the Rockets in seven games. The series was critically assailed for its lackluster offense, for the inability of either team to score 100 points in any game. Debunking the mythic power of the New York market, national Nielsen ratings took a precipitous dive. The river of universal praise that flowed the NBA's way since the early eighties dried up. When the New York Rangers broke a fifty-four-year drought and won the Stanley Cup that same spring, hockey's ratings soared and *Sports Illustrated* hypothesized, altogether prematurely, that hockey was hot and the NBA was not. In its forecasting wisdom, the magazine somehow neglected to factor Jordan into the equation.

When he rejoined the Bulls in March 1995, long forgotten were those fifty-five regular-season wins of the previous season. Few would remember how Pippen had won more regular-season games without Jordan than Jordan had ever won without Pippen. When I suggested that Pippen never lived down his 1.8 seconds of petulance, never received the recognition he deserved, Cartwright disagreed. Maybe that was the case with reporters and fans and NBA marketers, not with him. Not with the team. "He was voted one of the top fifty players, wasn't he?" Cartwright said, referring to a league promotion for its fiftieth anniversary. "We all knew what Scottie meant. In those championship seasons, he was incredible, the impact he had, guarding everybody on the floor."

Pippen may have been incredible but Jordan was already immortal, his bronze likeness weighing a ton and standing eleven and one-half feet high outside the new United Center. The sculpture was unveiled on November 1, 1994, the night the Bulls threw Jordan what of course turned out to be a premature retirement party. It was an event that coincided with my promotion at the *Times* from national NBA reporter to the prestigious "Sports of the Times" roster, alongside Dave Anderson, George Vecsey, Ira Berkow, and William C. Rhoden. My first assignment was to cover a Jets football game at Indianapolis on Sunday, then go on to Chicago for the Tuesday night Jordan ceremony.

I set my travel itinerary, planning to fly to Chicago from Indianapolis on Monday afternoon but later had a change of heart. I wanted to be home for a Halloween block party with my sons, then five and one, even if it created a more hectic itinerary. I changed my plans, took the first flight home to New Jersey on Monday morning, spent the afternoon and evening with the kids, helped put them to sleep, and went downstairs to turn on the television. There was a special report on the news channels: A plane, American Eagle 4184, had crashed in northern Indiana that afternoon while circling to land at Chicago O'Hare in an icy rainstorm. It took a while before the numbing realization set in that this was the flight that I had originally planned to take from Indianapolis. For at least half an hour, I sat frozen on the couch, staring at the screen, trying to fathom how a simple choice in all likelihood spared me tragedy. In the ensuing years I have tried not to dwell on the alternative reality as much as I embraced and let myself be guided by the decision I made, family first. And, of course, those hours that separated my first two "Sports of the Times" columns and the flight I reluctantly took the following morning made for the spookiest Halloween of my life.

Landing on Tuesday morning, I picked up the *Chicago Tribune* to read in the taxi on the way downtown from O'Hare. The lead sports story happened to be on the jersey retirements of two Bears' greats, Gale Sayers and Dick Butkus, years and years after they'd left the sport. The long overdue ceremony took place at halftime of a Monday night game, in pretty much the same weather that the plane had gone down in, each legend given forty-five rain-soaked seconds at the mike before the Packers got on with a rout of the Bears. In contrast, Jordan's guest list for his nationally televised soiree on ESPN included Larry King, Woody Harrelson, Spike Lee, the comedy of Sinbad, and special musical guest Boyz II Men. Bobby Knight stopped by to crack a rare smile and call Jordan "the best player to play any game." Jordan's night—an ostentatious demonstration of pro basketball's emerging values—made Sayers's and Butkus's and even Larry Bird's look like bingo night at a nursing home, though few even believed that Jordan, thirty-one, was really retired. And when the skeptics were proved right, when he returned in the early spring of 1994 with two words heard round the world—"I'm back"—the ultimate basketball Beatle retook the stage and his audience, more than ever, became a mosh pit of unrestrained, and sometimes destructively blind, idolatry.

One of Jordan's motivations in resuming his career, he said, was to set a good example for the gimme-gimme Generation Xers who were entering the league with mammoth contracts and inflated egos and undoing much of the goodwill he had created with Magic and Bird and the assorted Dream Teamers. Not only did players such as Chris Webber and Larry Johnson seem to have little use for authority, they had less tolerance for democracy. To the emerging young NBA star, the team was more of a tribe and its leading man—typically determined by whose income was greatest—was its unquestioned warlord. The concept of multiple stars, or even two, coexisting in pursuit of a common cause, seemed lost on this new breed.

Jordan was correct in his assessment that young players were increasingly self-absorbed, but what he failed to recognize was his role in creating the problem. The *Chicago Tribune*'s Sam Smith didn't call his bestseller *The Jordan Rules* just because Detroit's Chuck Daly had fashioned a defense of that name. In Jordan's second go-round as basketball's one and only, he had leverage no player in any team sport had ever had, and used it, usually for the benefit of his ancillary earning power.

Unlike Magic, Jordan had never envisioned himself as an NBA ambassador, or acted the part. In his mind, he was his own business entity, his own brand, with his personal interests vigorously pursued by influential lobbyists like Nike and his entrenched superagent, David Falk. The only thing Jordan was ever criticized for during his career, however mildly, was for being unapologetically apolitical. He played it safe, down the middle, making sure to offend no one. When an African-American, Harvey Gantt, asked for an endorsement during one of his two unsuccessful U.S. Senate campaigns to unseat Jesse Helms back in Jordan's home state of North Carolina, Jordan was overheard to say, "Republicans buy shoes, too."

This was no more a crime than it was for any centrist businessman, but Jordan made it clear going all the way back to Barcelona that when he placed his hand over his heart, he was affirming his allegiance to Phil Knight as much, if not more, than to David Stern. That was part of his double-edged legacy, too. Younger stars, always watching, always listening, pledged themselves to their corporate sponsors often before they signed their first NBA contract. There was a new daddy to please, another agenda to pursue.

Not long after Jordan's comeback, the intramural mimicry unfolded in grand playoff fashion during a 1995 second-round series between Chicago and Orlando—or Jordan's Universal against Shaquille O'Neal's Disney. On a Sunday afternoon in the bowels of Chicago's brand-new United Center, Stern cornered Brian McIntyre, the league's vice president for public relations. He wanted to know why reporters were making such a fuss in the pressroom following a Bulls' victory. McIntyre explained that Jordan had begun another media boycott. He wasn't talking to any credentialed person who didn't answer to the name of his good friend, Ahmad Rashad. Why? Jordan was apparently miffed by criticism regarding his jersey switch from the number forty-five he had begun his comeback with to his original and famed twenty-three.

He had originally said he'd taken the new number and retired twenty-three to honor his dead father. A rush of consumers to sportswear outlets for the forty-five jerseys that happened to be available ensued, by some miracle of manufacturing, for Jordan's return. But after a dismal playoff night in Orlando, Jordan reversed field, decided he needed the power of twenty-three. Never mind the fact that it was against league rules to capriciously switch numbers, or that the jersey-buying public had jammed the Bulls' switchboards to complain about being duped by Jordan and his merchandizing mafia. As if that messy situation wasn't bad enough, O'Neal had decided that if Jordan didn't have to share his postgame musings, why did he? "Happy Mother's Day," was the big man's postgame contribution to the sports pages of America. To his credit, Stern took the time to hear out protesting reporters, but all he could ultimately offer was, "Our guys have always been the best at this. No Steve Carltons here." Stern left us to interview Bulls' scrubs Steve Kerr and Will Perdue, while Jordan dressed in his private sanctum, having set another fine example for America's basketball youth.

You couldn't blame the young ones for worshipping the ground Jordan set his Nikes on, not after he had unlocked the vault of once-unfathomable corporate riches, empowered the modern athlete, and, especially, the African-American athlete on Madison Avenue. Not that his predecessors hadn't tried. In Monte Carlo, Magic Johnson told reporters of how he had, early in his career, begged Converse to market a basketball shoe in his very famous name. "They told me, 'No basketball player could ever sell a shoe,'" he said, "and then along came Michael." Along came the man who forgot about the spoils and the sycophants the moment he stepped inside the lines, who was unquestionably the

Bulls' dictator, but who in time learned that his larger legacy depended on his benevolence with the ball. The same could not often be said of those who followed, who wanted to be like Mike but too often misidentified Jordan's spoils for success and were impaled by the double-edged sword of his legacy.

5

1994: The Young and the Restless

IN THE YEAR that Michael Jordan briefly departed the NBA playoff stage, much of the American sports industry took leave of its senses. What began with a scandalous figure-skating story on the eve of the 1994 Winter Olympics—the repulsive assault most commonly remembered as *Nancy and Tonya*—continued with a National Hockey League lockout, and climaxed during the summer with a deleterious baseball strike that resulted in the historic cancellation of the World Series.

Repercussions from that year reverberated for the remainder of the decade, carrying over into the twenty-first century. Hockey never resolved its economic predicament and paid a catastrophic price for it in 2004–05 with the first cancellation of an entire professional sports season in the history of North America. Baseball made a deal with the devil to replenish its reservoir of public goodwill by launching a home-run era we know was perpetrated and fueled by chemically enhanced fakes (and in stark contrast to the quick condemnation of black basketball players for stepping out of line, the mainstream media were largely silent for a decade while baseball's Popeyes defrauded the public by spiking their spinach).

Yet, during the nineties, a decade that even saw the meteoric rise of professional wrestling, a pseudosport pumped up to levels of brain-rattling rage, there were broad economic lessons to be learned from the rise in popularity white-bread figure skating experienced following the Nancy Kerrigan kneecapping, however repellent the act. There was a message in those megamillions generated by assaults on baseball's home-run records, cheered by critics who should have known better: Do whatever you must to win. Subvert the rules. Thrash your opponent. Flaunt your good fortune. Flex for the camera. It'll make you a star on ESPN.

Pro basketball's contribution to the new culture of disrespect of everyone but your agent and accountant was the NBA's collective of dribbling emissaries known as Dream Team II to the World Championships. Originally scheduled for war-torn Yugoslavia, the August 1994 competition was moved to Toronto by FIBA, the international basketball federation, in what amounted to a scratch-my-back arrangement with David Stern. The NBA was a year away from launching its Canadian invasion with franchises in Toronto and Vancouver, and what better promotional bang could it get than another international lovefest starring the world's most renowned dunkaholics? Except for one thing: Gone were Michael, Magic, and Larry. In their place, among others, were Larry Johnson, Derrick Coleman, and Shawn Kemp.

Not that the entire team was made up of the young and the restless. The backcourt happened to be a delightful blend of veteran leadership and marksmanship, headed by Joe Dumars, Mark Price, Kevin Johnson, and Reggie Miller. Spike Lee's verbal sparring partner joined the Pacers in 1987, but his mouthy persona allowed him to bridge the gulf between the Happy Days eighties and the emerging MTV edginess of this new class. "It's a new era," Miller proclaimed one day after practice when the team was already under fire for behavior deemed unbecoming or downright antisocial. "Traditional basketball, when a guy dunked and just ran down court, that's gone."

In its place, apparently, was the license to jam and, while play was shifting to the other side of the court, preen for the camera, and caress one's self from face down to waist. That was how Larry Johnson celebrated in the midst of one U.S. rout, while Kemp took the feel-yourself-to-feel-good technique to an even lower common denominator: His slams were punctuated with a hearty crotch grab—his way of letting us know that if the game were played with two balls, he'd be dunking the second one, too.

"How does it hurt the other team?" Miller wanted to know. He contended that the young NBA players were not going out of their way to embarrass anyone, no matter what it looked like. Johnson, Kemp, and even Shaquille O'Neal were just expressing themselves, being playful, only more demonstratively than their predecessors. It was the way they'd been conditioned to compete, in places white sportswriters didn't understand and couldn't relate to, and an attitude that assisted them in surviving the dog-eat-dog NBA. Miller correctly reminded us that trash-talking was not the invention of the modern black player, that even good old French Lick country boy Bird had by the height of his career developed the knack for getting into an opponent's head. (I could vouch for that, having sat in Boston Garden one afternoon, watching him taunt the normally composed Julius Erving into an altercation.)

It was true that selective memories tended to obfuscate the original Dream Team's rambunctious side, from Barkley's hammering of the skinny Angolan to Karl Malone's bashing of Communists to Jordan's expedient tribute to the stars and stripes. But, as Donny Nelson had said, most people recognized that the original Dream Team players believed it was a privilege to represent the United States on a grand global stage. Most of its players didn't appreciate Barkley's foolishness, however lighthearted, and publicly said so. They respected the earnestness of their overmatched competitors, acknowledged the obstacles they were dealing with. Even a cutthroat competitor like Jordan showed compassion after one Dream Team rout. He sought out Antonio Diaz Miguel, the Spanish coach of twenty-seven years, who was under fire for having lost the previous game by 20 to Angola. Against the United States, Miguel was booed unmercifully for leaving the court at halftime. Jordan, who knew Miguel through Dean Smith, wanted to diffuse the situation, so he wrapped his arm around the Spaniard, and together they walked off.

Once Magic, Jordan, and company had planted the NBA flag in the heart of Europe, what exactly was the mission for those who followed? Sell more shoes and jerseys? Win by even larger scores? Measured against the originals, was it possible for them to really ever win? Andrew Gaze, an Australian guard who had played against many of Dream Team II players when he rented himself out to Seton Hall in the late 1980s, pinpointed the fundamental problem following a 130–74 drubbing in Toronto in which he and his teammates were run ragged, shot full of holes, disdainfully dunked on, laughed at, and repeatedly cursed. "The first Dream Team had something extra," Gaze said. "Those were the guys whose posters were in your room. These guys, I guess they're trying to prove something out there."

Their attitudes seemed to say: If you won't beg us for a photo op, we'll go ahead and posterize *you*. Dominance wasn't enough. They had to flog the competition like boot camp Marines, haze them like college fraternity pledges. Don Nelson, the U.S. coach, urged them to calm down, just play. He was virtually ignored and finally gave up. "Some of these guys can't control it," Nelson said. Stern and other league officials listened to the soundtrack of their young diplomats and winced. The league obviously recognized its edgier MTV appeal to younger fans, and that many apparently didn't mind the players straddling the line between flamboyance and vulgarity.

The international arena was something quite different, however. Cultural and social barriers were being crossed. Embracing the context of the mission was crucial to making a good impression, and yet the young players carried on like it was their typical NBA funhouse, oblivious to the fact that many of the foreign players were not wealthy professionals, nor even professionals, and were from places that knew little or no peace or prosperity. As if to underscore this point, a Cuban player disappeared from his team and delegation during the tournament and showed up hours later in the company of a Cuban expatriate and Toronto businessman. The player, a six-six center named Richard Matienzo, announced to a Toronto newspaper that he was defecting with nothing but the clothes—basketball shorts, T-shirt, and sneakers—he was wearing.

The following day, I contacted the Toronto businessman and arranged an interview with Matienzo, who said he had considered defecting nine months earlier in Ponce, Puerto Rico, but had not been able to muster the courage to leave behind his young son, pregnant girlfriend, and mother. Matienzo said he had no education beyond tenth grade and earned the equivalent of a few dollars a month playing ball for the state. The family lived in a one-room shack and struggled just to eat. Before he had left for Toronto, Matienzo's family begged him to defect, so he could go to college on a basketball scholarship and eventually earn money to send them. His mother told him she would kill herself if he came home.

That afternoon, I wrote about the defection and returned in the evening to the arena, where I began to realize that other great human interest stories were more worthy of space in the newspaper than the obnoxious Americans. Croatia was playing Russia in the semifinals, albeit without its best player and captain, Drazen Petrovic, who had died in June 1993 in a car accident on a German autobahn. The tragedy, on the eve of the Bulls-Suns Finals, shocked the NBA and especially those of us who knew the Nets' brash twenty-eight-year-old shooting guard. Petrovic wasn't the league's first European import but he was the first who crossed the Atlantic with higher hopes than just fitting in. Signed by Portland in 1990, Petrovic was proud of his basketball heritage and determined to prove that a European could make it big in the United States.

Traded to the Nets during the 1990–91 season, Petrovic became their leading scorer, a dead-eyed, long-range assassin, making more than 50 percent of his shots while averaging more than 22 points per game during the 1992–93 season, pouring in a game high of 44. Many were surprised when Petrovic was not voted by the coaches to be a reserve on the Eastern Conference All-Star team that season. He was shocked, according to Danny Ainge, a former Portland teammate whom he confided in. "He felt that his nationality had something to do with it," said Ainge, who agreed.

Petrovic's belief, which he never made public, suggested that the globally ambitious NBA wasn't as worldly and open-minded as it liked to think. While Hakeem Olajuwon had come from Nigeria and Detlef Schrempf from Germany to excel in the NBA, they had done so through the American college system. Sarunas Marciulionis had found a welcome home as a complementary player with the Warriors in the San Francisco Bay Area, and the Lakers' Vlade Divac broke in under Magic Johnson's wing. Only Petrovic was trying to elbow his way into the company of the NBA elite. Only he seemed to have the ego to match his talent, but many players, some of them his Nets teammates, resented Petrovic's attempts to impose his will on games, on his team. Where did this headstrong white boy from a country with fewer people than Chicago, with his marine buzz cut and comical brand of English, come off acting like some kind of star?

This conflict of cultures came to a head before a game against the Knicks in the New Jersey Meadowlands, when the Knicks' equally mouthy shooting guard, John Starks, lined up alongside Petrovic for the opening tap, determined to get into the Croat's head. Starks accused Petrovic of complicity in the first World Trade Center bombing. Ridiculous an insult as it was, Petrovic did not see the humor in any gratuitous invocation of war, not when Serbian bombs were falling on his homeland. By the time the game was over, Starks was in the Knicks locker room, shaking his head, calling Petrovic "a trash-talker with an accent."

Breaking new ground in any sport was daunting, as African-Americans have learned the hard way, although Petrovic and the early Europeans in the NBA were probably dealing more with cultural typecasting than racism, the way Russian and Swedish hockey stars did coming to North America. As the mid-nineties approached, NBA rosters were roughly 80 percent black, as were virtually all of its leading men. Bird, the reluctant torch carrier for white America, was gone, without a replacement in sight. At the highest levels, the sport seemed to be moving beyond the reach of white America—at least that was the message disseminated to both races. Young African-American players were bombarded with media proclamations of their dominance, supported by cultural explications such as the comic Hollywood hit, *White Men Can't Jump*. It was one thing for a screenwriter or a court jester like Charles Barkley to lampoon the white man's hops. Trying to explain the sport's evolution in a more serious way required wading into deeper sociological waters.

Pop cultural clichés notwithstanding, Dr. Richard Lapchick had spent more than three decades arguing that black dominance in basketball was no more physiological than it was in its segregated days, when tough Jewish kids from the city named Sy, Sonny, and Red ruled the courts. "For years scientists argued that blacks were built to run short distances, not long," said Lapchick, director of the Institute for Diversity and Ethics in Sport at the University of Central Florida. "Then we had all these marathons won by Africans. I'm not saying blacks and whites are exactly the same but I believe the better explanation for what happened with basketball in this country tells us more about how we play the game, the assumptions made by white athletes that if they want to play a sport seriously, they need look elsewhere. A disproportionate amount of African-Americans have pursued the game more intensely," as a means to an economic end.

White Americans became trapped in the same cycle of negativity, Harry Edwards argued, as blacks in, for example, politics. "They look at a black league and say, 'I can't compete,'" Edwards said. "The same if you're black and you look at the Senate and see all white. You're probably not going to think you can be a senator." A sampling of my own community supported these contentions. Montclair, New Jersey, a town of thirty-nine thousand about twelve miles west of the Lincoln Tunnel, featured public schools nationally recognized for their racial diversity. Its playing fields tended to look quite different, being only marginally integrated. Black children easily outnumbered whites on youth football and basketball teams, while soccer and lacrosse fields and hockey rinks resembled those of predominantly white suburbs.

Athletes, living and competing in the moment, are not social scientists. With the few American white players cast more than ever as role players, with the game embracing black culture in look and sound, why wouldn't African-American players initially greet the white foreign-born stars skeptically, especially after what they'd seen during the summer of Barcelona? Why wouldn't Jordan and Pippen have been baffled by Jerry Krause's lust to land Petrovic's Croatian teammate, Toni Kukoc, the so-called European Magic Johnson, and pay a steep price to pry him away from the rich Italian club, Benetton Treviso. When Kukoc took the floor against the Dream Team in Barcelona, Jordan and Pippen pounced on the opportunity to make life miserable for the unsuspecting young Croat, harassing him into an embarrassing audition.

Kukoc regained his composure and played creditably in the gold-medal game, and Krause brought him to Chicago during the '93 playoffs to take a physical before signing a contract with the Bulls. Having never been to an NBA game, Kukoc flew all the way from Europe but wouldn't so much as step into the arena to watch his future team play the Knicks. Krause said Kukoc told him he did not want to be a distraction. Jordan and Pippen's problems with Kukoc probably had more to do with their contempt for Krause, but there wasn't a kid in America who would have been made to feel that unwelcome, who wouldn't have slipped a Bulls cap on his head, taken a bow.

During those months, Petrovic was aware of what Kukoc was experiencing, and, while he was named third-team all-league by the voting media, he was still smarting from the All-Star Game snub. With his New Jersey contract expiring, there was speculation that he was considering packing up, returning to Europe.

Petrovic never got to make his decision. His death devastated the Croatian basketball community, and gave the war-ravaged country one more reason to mourn.

In Toronto, my seat at the press table happened to be a couple of feet from the Croatia bench for its semifinal game with Russia, in effect, for the silver medal as neither team was planning on beating the United States for the gold. Before the game, I noticed a familiar face behind the bench, a fellow named Mario Miocic, who had been Petrovic's close friend, his confidant, and link to New York's Croat community. A restaurant worker from the Adriatic coastal town of Zadar, thirty-five miles from Petrovic's native Sibenik, Miocic immigrated to the United States in 1986 and became something of a one-man Croat chamber of commerce for athletes like Petrovic, Dino Radja, and the tennis star, Goran Ivanisevic, when they came to compete in the States.

Out of habit and loyalty, Miocic continued attending Nets games after the tragedy. With a nod of approval from the Nets' front office, he camped in the runway leading to the locker rooms, a white pin with Petrovic's retired jersey number, three, fastened to his lapel. On the night of the Nets' last game of the 1993–94 season, I wrote a column chronicling Miocic's long season of tribute, his relief as it ended, allowing him a more personal closure. When he spoke of Petrovic, there were tears in his eyes. "Drazen used to tell me, 'I never think, "Oh, good, I've opened the door to European players and now I am going to sit on the bench and be happy,"'" Miocic told me. (Eight years later, Petrovic was posthumously elected to the Basketball Hall of Fame. Miocic, relocated to Florida, called to share the news, to reminisce. He asked if I thought that the Europeans starring in the league—Dirk Nowitzki, Peja Stojakovic, Pau Gasol—were all a tribute to his friend Drazen. I told him, yes, they were part of the Hall of Fame legacy.)

Before the semifinal in Toronto tipped off, Miocic let me in on a bittersweet story: Two of the players, Dino Radja and Stojan Vrankovic, were planning to take their silver medals home to present to Petrovic's family. But the heartwarming saga dissolved when Croatia lost by two points to Russia, a team with no NBA players, another small sign that everyone was improving. The Croats cried on the bench, Miocic right along with them. The plight and poignancy of the international teams became the tournament's saving grace.

Led by O'Neal, the Americans won the gold, as promised, walloping the competition by an average of 38 points per game, only five short of the original Dream Team margin. By the end of the competition, however, the foreign players had had enough of the preening Americans. "They better behave themselves," Aussie Andrew Gaze presciently warned. "Sooner or later, there will be teams that could shut them up."

There was one glimpse into the future during the tournament, as the Russians stubbornly hung with the Americans early into the second half. Following one Russian surge to the lead, Don Nelson jumped off the bench and did what Chuck Daly had not once done in Barcelona. Timeout, U.S.A. The Russians marched off to their bench smug with satisfaction. "Top-notch but definitely human," snapped their coach, Sergei Belov, who knew vulnerability when he sniffed it. Belov had been on the floor when the Russians defeated the United States for the first time in Munich. "Sooner or later, someone will give this team a fight," he predicted.

For the time being, the international basketball arena remained an American bully pulpit, even as Stern promised by the tournament's end to rein in his young. He had grown up watching the likes of Earl Monroe, Oscar Robertson, and Sam Jones, all players who believed it was cool to be calm. On the day of the gold medal game, Stern stood behind the stands of the Toronto SkyDome, admitting he didn't like the churlish behavior and promising a team of adults for the next Olympics, in 1996. Little did Papa Stern suspect that his babysitting days had only just begun.

6

1995: School Daze

WHILE THE HALLOWED LOCKER ROOMS of the NBA were experiencing the early stages of the foreign invasion, the league was also, by mid-decade, hearing another knock on its increasingly creaky door. After filing my column on Jordan's Mother's Day media boycott that was imitated by Shaquille O'Neal following the Bulls-Orlando playoff game at the United Center on May 15, 1995, my office called and asked me to lay over an extra day. A Chicago high-school player had scheduled a press conference for the following afternoon, and the word was that he was going to announce something most people believed he'd regret: Kevin Garnett, a name I'd never heard, was going to skip college and declare himself eligible for the NBA draft.

While players were routinely leaving college early, on the basis of a 1971 Supreme Court decision that overturned the NBA rule closing out those who had not been out of high school four years, rare was the Moses Malone, the prodigy who dared to make the preps-to-pros jump. Whom did Garnett call for advice before making his decision? Bill Willoughby, who was often cited as the earliest flop of down-underclassmen, though he did salvage an eight-year career as an NBA journeyman. Yet, by consulting a player who had not succeeded on a grand scale, Garnett was already demonstrating a knack for thinking outside the box.

Willoughby told the six-eleven string bean to go for it because if he wasn't planning on going to college for the long haul, what was the point?

The Garnett press conference was held at a well-known Chicago pizza joint and sports pub, the Home Run Inn. The room was crowded with Chicago basketball insiders, reporters from major newspapers, and, of course, Garnett's homeroom homeys from Farragut Academy on the city's blighted West Side. They cheered him on as he talked the talk, declaring himself ready to "step up" and go to the "next level," and especially when he took on the question of impending millionaire bachelorhood by rolling his eyes and hips. "Come on, ladies," Garnett intoned. "Come on."

The press conference was not unlike a stage show from the school of performing arts, a kid imitating what he'd watched on television. In fact, Ron Eskridge, an assistant coach at Farragut Academy, said Garnett's ambition was "to go to the NBA and have Nike name a shoe after him." If ever there was proof that the Jordan Rules were now firmly established as the law of the basketball land, here it was. I asked Eskridge if any NBA teams had scouted Garnett during the one season he played Chicago high-school ball after falling into the clutches of the Nike body snatchers and moving up from Mauldin, South Carolina. He looked at me as if I had three heads and said, by his unofficial count, twenty-three. So why, he asked, would Garnett or any other eighteen-year-old in his position put himself through the NCAA crosshairs for a year or two when the NBA was holding its arms out to him now?

In the predictable firestorm that followed, Stern was quick to defend his teams, swatting away the charge that the NBA was committing a heinous act by accelerating the breakdown of educational values. Stern wanted to know why few people, if any, called it a violation of the social contract when the typical teenage tennis sensation was whisked from his or her home and enrolled in one of those Sun Belt boarding schools that looked like a giant hard court. "Where was the outrage for Martina Hingis, for Chris Evert, for Jimmy Connors?" Stern said when I called him for a 1996 column comparing two young sensations in the process of forsaking college—basketball's Kobe Bryant and tennis's Justin Gimelstob.

Gimelstob, a North Jersey kid who quit UCLA after his freshman year as the country's number-one-ranked collegian to join the tour, was from a sports family better known around gymnasiums than tennis courts. His uncle, Jerry, was a longtime Bob Knight assistant at Indiana and later the head coach at George Washington University. His father, Barry, had coached three high-school basketball state champions in Newark. When I interviewed Barry Gimelstob for my column, we had a long discussion on Garnett's leap of faith, and the precedent it had set for Bryant and others, undoubtedly. Barry Gimelstob noted that the only high-school players who had bypassed college and succeeded in the NBA were big men. Wasn't this Kobe Bryant a shooting guard, he asked? I said, yes, he was. "He has no chance," Gimelstob said.

Gimelstob's poor prognosticative skills were not so much the problem as was his insistence, after decades of conditioning, that college was the only way to raise a professional basketball player. As a rookie in Minnesota, Kevin Garnett was no instant sensation but he was far from the undernourished and hopeless novice many believed he'd be. Garnett played in eighty games and averaged more than twenty-eight minutes. He scored 10 points per game and made a shade below 50 percent of his shoots. He grabbed 501 rebounds and blocked 131 shots. Granted, Garnett was a special case, mature for his age, even more so than some of his fellow rookies who had apprenticed for a year or two at the NCAA basketball factories.

He demonstrated that one night at the rookie orientation program, a four-day tutorial the league holds every September in conjunction with the players union. The league agreed to allow me, on assignment for the *Times,* to sit in on some of the events, including one in which a professional acting troupe staged a variety of life-situation skits to test the players' coping skills. In one, a fictitious player named Marvin Davis portrayed an NBA point guard whose drug-addict brother constantly begs him for cash.

"They'll kill me," the brother pleaded, on his knees, referring to his dealers. "Do you know what that would do to Mama?" The actors froze. A moderator appeared. He wanted to know what the rookies thought of the brother in need. Only Garnett, the high-school player, took a shot. "He's a junkie," he said. The moderator reminded him, "But he's Marvin's brother." Garnett shrugged and snorted, "He's still a junkie," precisely the answer the actors were seeking, the recognition of how wealthy young athletes become natural targets to be exploited. This Garnett kid had a flair about him, but, as Bryant and others took note of his immediate success, it was certainly fair to wonder how emotionally prepared most eighteen-year-olds were for itinerant NBA life, for the professional and personal pressures of the fast lane, and the "come on" ladies waiting out on the road.

"The problem as I see it is that the NBA doesn't have anything in place, a support system to help these kids once they get there," Arlene Daag, a Farragut assistant principal, told me on the day Garnett turned pro at the Home Run Inn. Here was an experienced educator, a woman who had no vested interest in Garnett's success, getting right to the heart of the matter. She wasn't mouthing the platitudes of a quasicollege education as much as she was endorsing Garnett's right to play professionally already granted him by the Supreme Court. She just wanted to know what the NBA, after scouting him and stamping him as first-round worthy, would provide as a support system. A rookie orientation program wasn't enough. The NBA had to stop treating the NCAA as its de facto minor league and start investing in its own developmental vehicle.

History tells us that Garnett's press conference was a watershed moment for the basketball industry, the dawning of a new reality. In my column the following day, I hit on a theme that would become a staple of my writings for the next decade: "Kevin Garnett thinks he's ready for the NBA. Is the NBA ready for him? Maybe it needs to start thinking about creating its own developmental system. Stern and Company have gotten a free ride, using the colleges as a de facto minor league system, receiving its well-coached, highly publicized products. Now the trend appears to be that these kids are stopping off at the university for a year, maybe two, if at all."

While Stern had effectively used Chris Evert and Jimmy Connors to defend Garnett, and was still invoking tennis stars a decade later to rail against the double standard for young black males, they were not appropriate comparisons. The average American tennis pro was from a middle- to upper-middle-class family and the typical career clock—most players were finished before thirty—made conventional high school as much a deterrent as college. Why did no one in the media or in the university network ever challenge the wisdom of the young baseball player who passes on the scholarship for the professional scratch? Where was the bereavement, the programmed political correctness, for the baseball player who spurned Arizona State or the rink rat that skated right into hockey's minor leagues instead of taking the full ride to Michigan or another NCAA hockey power?

Why did no one lecture J. M. Gold of Toms River, New Jersey, that he was making the mistake of his life when he turned down a full ride to St. John's in 1998 to sign a lucrative deal with the Milwaukee Brewers as the thirteenth pick of baseball's amateur draft? "Any kid who is drafted in the first round of any sport is going to be offered a lot of money," said Gold's father, Larry, a tractor-trailer driver for a supermarket chain. When I called him for the purpose of comparing options and ideologies of the two sports, Larry Gold told me that his most fervent wish was for all three of his sons to go to college. But when his middle son, Jon-Michael, said he wanted to turn pro, all he could do was give him his blessing and a hug.

As an eighteen-year-old, J. M. Gold played rookie league ball in Ogden, Utah, where he lived in the small-town custody of a local family and paid his dues on long bus rides to places like Billings and Butte. There were no guarantees of a storybook ride to the major leagues and, in fact, Gold suffered several arm injuries and was released by the Brewers organization in 2004. It was his decision, though, his right to try. But there was no Billy Packer in baseball, no Dick Vitale, to seize on his misfortune and pontificate on television that he should have taken the scholarship, gone to St. John's. Nobody played the education card to hide their true agenda for one reason: There wasn't enough money to make on college baseball players to make it worth their while.

If attending a major university was no longer seen as critical for entry and ensuring success as an NBA player, the college basketball experience also warranted a thorough examination of its own sloppy terms. For it was there, within the purported sanctuary of academia and amateur sport, that the origins of the divisions between players and fans could be found. It was in the college arena where the cancer of basketball's racial typecasting and its eventual carryover to the punitively scrutinized pro level took root.

A couple of weeks after the Pistons-Pacers brawl at The Palace of Auburn Hills, I stumbled upon a provocative article while surfing the Web. It was written for *PopMatters,* an Internet journal of cultural criticism, by Mark Anthony Neal, an associate professor of African and African-American studies at Duke. Not wasting any time revealing his intentions, Neal entitled the piece: "The Real Nigger Show."

He began by saying that he happened to be reading a 1986 book by Joseph Boskin called *Sambo: The Demise of An American Jester,* during a week in which three separate but related pop cultural events served, in his opinion, to eviscerate the book's premise. Boskin, according to Neal, wrote that in the nineteenth and early twentieth centuries, Sambo was a symbol of an overtly racist society, presented in a variety of forms, including stage performers, artifacts, and athletes, "to make the black into an object of laughter . . . to strip him of his masculinity, dignity and self-possession." To which Neal wrote: "Yeah, maybe Sambo did die, but there's been a resurrection." He cited the opening segment of the previous week's *Monday Night Football* broadcast that featured Nicollette Sheridan of *Desperate Housewives* shedding the towel covering her birthday suit and leaping into the arms of the Philadelphia Eagles' Terrell Owens; the rap-heavy Vibe Award ceremony on UPN that included an inaugural video-ho award; and the granddaddy of them all, the instantly infamous eruption and territorial escalation of violence in suburban Detroit between the Pistons and the Pacers, live on ESPN.

These episodes, Neal wrote, were "proof that Sambo and the minstrel stage that so powerfully nurtured his existence are still alive and well." More specifically, on the fight, he added: "The heightened visibility of highly paid black male athletes has helped create an industry of derision—sports talk radio being just one example—and indeed such derision, even hatred, is the price for black male athletes who desire to be those highly visible, highly priced bucks. In an effort to keep their fandom happy and paying . . . owners of professional sports teams and sports commentators often turn a blind eye to the rhetorical violence that black male athletes face and the threats of real violence that fester beneath the surface, not unlike that which exploded in Detroit."

This was not exactly the oratory I would have expected from Duke's ivory towers of gentility, but the singular condemnation of professional sports owners as facilitators of minstrelsy was troubling. There was no question pro sports and specifically the NBA, with its itinerant culture of temptation, contributed to stereotypes and caricatures. Yet it wasn't enough to just blame Stern's league, any more than it was to suggest that the objectionable-to-criminal behavior of some players was a direct result of their sudden wealth. While it was clear to me that professional basketball players were the most scrutinized and harshly judged athletes in America, I was also fairly certain this was in large part a systemic byproduct of an industry that, far from a nurturing environment, spoiled and exploited these boys-to-men long before they became dribbling mercenaries.

It wasn't the NBA that was in the business of targeting players when they were thirteen and fourteen years old, scouting them through the AAU system, which over the years has become travel basketball on steroids, a labyrinth of wheelers and dealers funded in part by the shoe companies whose payrolls just happened to include most big-time college coaches. Though it represented the ultimate payday, the basketball Oz, it wasn't the NBA that was endorsing the year-round obsession with the game, distorting the social and academic development of preadolescents by turning them into pimply road warriors. "One day I'm checking into the Fairmont Hotel in Chicago, a pretty posh hotel," Chuck Daly told me. "I turn around and there's an AAU team checking in. I asked how old the kids were. They were twelve. Twelve-year-olds checking into the Fairmont! I said to myself, 'What have we created?' "

When I contacted Professor Neal to raise these counterpoints to his article, I was relieved to hear that he was no Cameron Crazy, no blind college-basketball cheerleader who believed in the purity of the so-called amateur athletic mission based on Duke's largely acceptable graduation levels. Here was one sports-loving academic, raised in the Bronx, who wasn't arguing, as Duke's Mike Krzyzewski and many of the big-time coaches so often did, that a fully paid college education was the birthright for every kid, minority and otherwise, who could dunk and shoot the three.

"That's a dicey issue around here, because the Duke players are generally thought of as being more accomplished than at North Carolina State and Wake Forest," Neal said. "But several players have also left Duke early the last few years so even on our campus, there is a tremendous effort that goes into recruiting the top players and then even more in trying to keep them in school. The connection I make is to the plantation: How do you keep these kids on it? When they come, people ask, do they have the right to be here? When they go, it becomes, why aren't they grateful? When you set up a system in that context and then come up on the other side with multimillion dollar contracts, that adds to the sense of these kids being undeserving, ungrateful, unwilling to be educated. That creates an ongoing judgment on the performance of blackness." Neal made the clear connection the pious defenders of the college game couldn't, or wouldn't: Long before they collected an NBA paycheck, it was in the big-time college sports arena where the portrayal of black men as athletic minstrels began.

College basketball people preferred to make the NBA the target of their frustration, blame Stern for raiding their talent pool, for corrupting the young with gobs of cash. Billy Packer, the most tenured network cheerleader, seldom passed on the opportunity to launch a few shots at Big Brother, portraying the NBA as an ethically challenged circus and a bastardized brand of ball. He chided Stern for bleeding corporate welfare from budget-strapped cities for luxury-box-endowed arenas, somehow forgetting the taxpayer money that went into the construction of state university stadiums, arenas, and weight rooms.

At least the NBA wasn't hiding what it was, a purely for-profit enterprise. Packer and company typically avoided the subject of college basketball's molecular principles, the dysfunction it wallowed in due to the never-ending conflict between its high-minded ideals and its revenue-driven reality. As for what the college game was selling and to whom, you had to wonder if Packer had ever removed his headphones during a telecast and taken a good look around the typical Division I basketball fun house. Cheering or mocking the players, the majority of whom were African-American, were people not likely to cross campus paths with these ultrainsulated athletes, especially at the graduation the majority of players would never attend.

As the years have passed, as the scandalous tales of impropriety have been revealed, I have had difficulty separating the athletics from the academics, the pep rallies from the prep realities. Too often when the cameras scan the stands, I find myself asking, Do the kids with their faces painted the school colors really believe the players represent them? Do they view them as genuine peers or preening performers? Do those middle- and upper-middle-class kids comprise the next generation of corporate NBA courtside-ticket holders who will shower players they believe are undereducated and undeserving of their multimillions with boos and beer?

Wildly entertaining as the games can be, and were throughout the 2005 NCAA tournament, the sport had to ultimately be judged in the context of what too many Division I programs are about. As Duke professor Neal told me: "Minority kids carted out there for the entertainment benefit of the townies, the alumni, and the students from wealthier backgrounds." In other words, used, in far too many cases, to perpetuate an industry of profit-making and those less-quantifiable but even more significant benefits popular football and basketball programs bring: surges in student applications nationwide. As Fairleigh Dickinson coach Tom Green told *The New York Times* after his team qualified for the 2005 NCAAs, "Every admissions director has walked into my office the times we've made the tournament and has said: 'Congratulations. You just made my job easier.'"

Stalking the sidelines, these coaches are hailed as champions of social justice, dedicated teachers. Largely unspoken of on national television are the sad-sack graduation rates at the majority of Division I schools, the recruiting follies, the academic fraud. Most often the bad news leaks out like a dark political secret but, occasionally, in torrents of shame, as in the spring and summer of 2003, when real madness preceded and followed the NCAA tournament, when academic scandals unfolded in rapid-fire succession at the University of Georgia, Fresno State, and even little St. Bonaventure.

Bad as those firestorms were, they looked like brush fires compared to the unspeakable inferno several months later at Baylor University. The shooting death of a player, Patrick Dennehy, led to charges of murder against a teammate, Carlton Dotson, and subsequent revelations so sordid that even a legendary cynic of human nature like Tom Wolfe would have agreed were stranger than fiction: a lying, cheating, veteran coach—the woefully misnamed Dave Bliss—at the world's largest Baptist university, caught on tape by an assistant with a conscience, recruiting accomplices to help cast the dead man as a player in the drug world in an attempt to save his program.

Rather than shut down a program that had sunk to the depths of hell, Baylor hired a new coach and got on with the games. As was often the case, however, when the college game turned dirty or in this case, deadly, African-American males were again plastered across the headlines, cast in endless sports analysis as academic and societal losers, willing participants in a con or much worse. The process by which young black males were portrayed in America's local newscasts—typically in handcuffs—repeated itself. First came fear. Then came loathing. Or as Peter Roby of the Boston-based Center for the Study of Sport in Society told me: "Every time an African-American kid gets into trouble with the law or with the NCAA, it's another reason to say: They don't care, they can't learn."

Outside the arena, educators and social scientists can only lament the rabid recruitment of young men barely, if at all, on the university-ready bubble, eighteen-year-olds who are ill-prepared by underfunded, decrepit high schools expected to transform themselves into serious students while holding down what amount to full-time jobs, and under enormous pressure to justify and sustain their scholarships. In the process of this profit-seeking smoke screen, too often have the achievements of more serious student-athletes been obscured under the avalanche of bad news. Too often the mutually exclusive subjects of minority education and big-time college sports have become symbiotic issues thanks to the power of the sports culture. Too often have the advancements of nonathletic students been ignored.

In the 2004 March/April edition of *Futurist* magazine, Nat Irvin, assistant dean and executive professor at The Babcock Graduate School of Management at Wake Forest University, wrote that the high-school completion rate for African-Americans has increased from 68 to 76 percent over the past two decades. Between 1980 and 2000, the percentage of African-Americans between the ages of eighteen and twenty-four attending two- and four-year colleges rose to 37 percent for men and 43 percent for women. Who would know about the good news when black achievement is so often viewed through the sports lens, when the media is so fixated on the prize recruit's ability to produce the required SAT score for a year or two of eligibility at Exploit U?

"I know there is something happening in the black community reflecting an understanding of the need to compete academically, although it too often is overshadowed by sports and that pisses me off," said Irvin, who is also the founder of Future Focus 2020, dedicated to bringing futurist thinking to urban and minority communities. Several times I have visited inner-city classrooms to meet kids who disassemble computers, not opposing defenses, and for whom arranging the financial college puzzle is practically a full-time job. Many are destined to drop out under the unprivileged weight of young adulthood, but who, with access to the newspapers and airwaves, makes the case for the poor urban non-dribbler, struggling earnestly and financially to make the grade? To those kids' teachers, "Coach's" faux idealism does not add up, or compute. "The colleges hire these athletes to do a job," Jane Silverstein, with four decades in as a teacher of honors math and science students at Paterson, New Jersey's inner-city Kennedy High School, told me. "They're on the college payroll."

The self-importance of college basketball coaches, their delusional belief in themselves as committed educators, was always difficult to take and reached comical heights at a 2001 conclave in Kansas City in the attempt to create a game plan for self-reform. Working under the banner of the National Association of Basketball Coaches, the coaches and administrators suggested: "Wherever it is not unduly awkward that coaches be referred to as teacher-coaches in the same manner as players are called student-athletes." Thankfully, this absurd measure never gained traction, as the majority of programs continued to graduate players at the approximate rate that Harvard turned out gangsta rappers.

In a study of 2005 men's tournament teams conducted by the respected sports industry watchdog, Richard Lapchick for the Institute for Diversity and Ethics in Sport at the University of Central Florida, forty-two of the sixty-four teams were said to have graduated fewer than 50 percent of basketball players admitted from 1994 through 1997 over a period of six years. Twenty schools were under 30 percent and two, Minnesota and LSU, graduated none. The aforementioned Fairleigh Dickinson, a school with no chance to win a national championship, with no players leaving early for the NBA, made life easier for its admissions people while sending 11 percent of its players off with degrees. "A continuing nightmare," Lapchick called the results, while emphasizing the sizable achievement gap existing between white students and black.

Every March, the media machine, ignoring these sad truths, cranks up the hard sell of the NCAA tournament. Announcer Dick Vitale can be counted on to remind the McDonald's All-Americans what they'd be missing if they turned pro. The excitement, baybee! The drama. And, of course, who wouldn't want to play in such an environment? Who wouldn't love to be deified on television? But the band didn't play on Monday morning. No one chanted your name on the way to class. The sport has been rife with players who were media savvy enough to know what middle-aged, mythologizing former frat boys wished to hear, wanted to write, only to declare their intention to go pro a few days after the Big Dance. These players knew the score, understood they lived in a parallel universe from the student body, and that their campus-hero status could disappear the moment they ran afoul of an arcane NCAA violation. Then they stood to be vilified by the same college communities that professed to love them.

"To tell you the truth, this is why kids are going to the NBA, because the situation with the high-school coaches and the AAU coaches and the college coaches—a lot of it gets out of hand," said the Lakers' forward Lamar Odom, a New York City native who spoke from experience. As a high-school senior, he attended three schools, a practice that had gained in popularity as players sought out comfort zones, often where there was no Coach Carter to burden them with excessive academic demands. An ill-fated courtship with UNLV produced only a citation for soliciting a prostitute and publicized suspicions that Odom's standardized test scores involved sleight of hand. On he went to Rhode Island, where he worked his way to passable academic standing only to have his one-season career screech to a halt when he hired an agent before he was sure he wanted to turn pro. That cost him his collegiate eligibility and earned him familiar media derision: another young African-American male who could not be counted on to do the right thing, even for himself.

College wasn't a total loss, Odom recalled. He got to play in one NCAA tournament, which earned the school a hefty bonus and vaulted his Rhode Island coach, Jim Harrick, to a more lucrative post at Georgia, where he proceeded to build a program that collapsed under the weight of academic fraud in 2003. Harrick's replacement at Rhode Island was a fellow named Jerry DeGregorio, who just happened to have been one of Odom's senior year high-school coaches. Odom's path to the pros was a classic microcosm of the amateur cesspool and why Spike Lee told me, "The coaches make the money. The kids get in trouble."

The mere mention of college basketball and its recruiting underworld of double-talking coaches, shoe company bagmen, and AAU climbers gave Lee the creeps. "These guys are pimps of the worst kind," he said, not bothering to differentiate one group from the other. "At least the pimps on the corner don't tell you, 'I've got you so I can get you an education.'" The sport still had its share of linchpins, its articulate icons, its Coach Ks. But beyond Xs and Os, the only lesson too many coaches taught their impressionable future pros was how to pump-fake their way out of a long-term contract. Career climbing is no crime, but in all of sports there are no bigger job-jumping weasels than college basketball coaches. They routinely sign lengthy deals, promise their recruits and their parents their unwavering support, then bolt at the first sniff of a higher-profile and -paying position.

Over the years I have been amazed by how easily sports writers could crucify the professional athlete for dishonoring a contract but give a free pass to Coach Ex when he excused himself from a long-term commitment. I asked Dr. Carol Cartwright, the president of Kent State and a strong reform advocate I occasionally consulted when addressing college sports, why schools seldom, if ever, held coaches to their signatures and even put interpretive language in the contracts allowing them out. Cartwright sighed when I expressed amazement that Stan Heath had left Kent State for Arkansas after one season (of five contracted) that produced a Cinderella run to the Sweet Sixteen, albeit with a team Heath inherited from the previous coach. "I think we all know we want to maintain the ability to recruit a new coach," she said. In other words, who wanted to be known as that rare university that just said no, that put the interests of its student-athletes ahead of its coach?

The flip side of the argument, the coaches' side, has been that their loyalty can never be reciprocal. For not winning, for not filling the arena, not pleasing the alumni, they get fired. Their jobs are not tenured. Then again, how many literature professors make hundreds of thousands of dollars a year and cash in on their positions as shoe-company pitchmen? By calling themselves victims of circumstance, forced to play the dirty hands they are dealt, they are also admitting that they are the sons of Frankenstein, wired and hired to justify the hefty investments in the program. Where is the educational mission in that?

If the schools cared so much about graduating basketball players, they wouldn't accept recruits they knew didn't belong and had almost no chance to succeed academically, given the year-round demands of being a Division I athlete. If the concerns of the coaches and the administrators were to maximize the players' chances to acclimate themselves as students, they would listen to old-school coaches like Dean Smith and Larry Brown, one of his North Carolina disciples, who have long advocated a return to the freshman ineligibility rule. "Coach Smith and I have talked about this," Brown said. "You wouldn't have freshmen under pressure to prove themselves, traveling all over the place. They'd have a year to learn fundamentals."

The way baseball forced kids to commit three years to college if they didn't turn pro out of high school, freshman ineligibility would quickly separate those really interested in school, in sacrificing for the scholarship, from those stopping by for a year or two of ESPN airtime, for an NBA audition. What educational and ethical justification was there for doling out scholarships on such terms? What did it say about the profession when a coach subjected himself to the worst kind of pandering, groveling on the living room carpet of Mr. Basketball to please, please grace the program, use it as a one-season stepping stone?

I have known Rick Pitino since he was Hubie Brown's thirty-ish assistant coach with the Knicks in the mid-1980s, admired him for his energy, his passion, and his ability to steer clear of academic scandal. In December of 2003, Pitino compassionately accompanied Francisco Garcia home to the Bronx after the star forward's brother was gunned down, but it was depressing when Pitino also found time on that trip to conspicuously camp out at the press table of a nationally televised high-school game on ESPN that featured a Brooklyn prodigy, Sebastian Telfair. Telfair, the cousin of Knicks point guard Stephon Marbury, had committed to Louisville, with the stipulation he'd turn pro given the assurances of being a first-round draft pick. Considering that his family was mired in the Coney Island projects, why would he have stayed around, risked blowing out his knee? How many coaches, who campaigned for kids to stay in college and postpone the windfall that would lift their families out of grinding poverty, exercised such patience when their own big offers materialized?

Pitino paid homage to Telfair because that was how Syracuse's Jim Boeheim finally won an NCAA championship after a lifetime on the job, by convincing Carmelo Anthony to surrender a year's pay and spend a couple of semesters in wintry upstate New York. The more NBA players who bypassed the big-time recruiting factories, the less centralization of power and money there could be in the college game, and the greater the odds were that a Division I titan such as Boeheim would find himself in his 2005 predicament, trying to explain a first-round NCAA tournament loss to a Lilliputian like Vermont.

Two years earlier, Boeheim and Syracuse got their precious title and Anthony his improved NBA draft status, but the begging and obliging had the predictable effect on the eighteen-year-old ego. By the time of his selection to the U.S. Olympic team for the 2004 Athens Games, Anthony's sense of self-worth was so inflated he couldn't accept a minor role in Larry Brown's rotation of NBA All-Stars. When Brown summoned Anthony to sub into a game after the outcome was decided, Anthony looked at him like he was speaking Lithuanian.

"You ever think about the guy who goes in for you?" Brown asked him. "He was probably a big star somewhere, too." No, Anthony replied, he hadn't given much thought to the scrubs that had allowed him to be feted by the crowd in the last minute or two. Anthony had always been the ascendant, not the apprentice, and that was why Brown believed, "There are some kids that have no interest in college and if they have no interest, to go to Georgetown with the idea of coming right out is stupid." His reasoning was simple: How could a kid have any grip on reality when so much effort went into having him for one year and pleasing him so that maybe, just maybe, he'd stick around for a second?

Many of these players may not be book smart but they sure aren't stupid. They came to recognize the hypocrisy of the terms of the agreement they'd made, the full-court press to keep them in a school they were unlikely to graduate from while their families struggled to make ends meet. As soon as Stephon Marbury knew the score, he passed on a second year at Georgia Tech. "When I signed to go to Georgia Tech, we were on ESPN like twenty times," he told me. "When you make the tournament, they just give [the school] money. And then they say a coach can't buy you a winter coat, even if you grew up in the 'hood and you don't have one. And then the coach gets a raise."

The money was real good, getting better. In December 2004, Connecticut announced that it had re-signed its NCAA defending champion coaches, Jim Calhoun and the women's guru, Geno Auriemma, to long-term contract extensions. Calhoun's salary was raised from $936,000 to $1.4 million, Auriemma to $825,000 from $665,000. How exactly was Calhoun worth more to Connecticut than Auriemma? Number of championship seasons? Auriemma had five national titles to Calhoun's two. Classroom achievement? During the 2004 double championship run, Richard Lapchick's study revealed Auriemma's program to be graduating at a rate of 67 percent, while Calhoun, who over the years has sent several talented underclassmen to the pros, weighed in at a wretched 27 percent. In a strict academic sense, a better case could be made for Calhoun's dismissal than for a substantial raise. Fat chance. Calhoun's teams were nationally renowned and he, with Boeheim, was voted into the Basketball Hall of Fame in early 2005. Inside the more moneyed men's bracket, life was good as a cash cow mouthing mantras of expediency.

In a Q & A with the *New York Post* during the 2005 Big East Tournament, Calhoun was asked if he had any interest in coaching an NBA team. "I like to control . . . mold a young guy as opposed to having to deal with corporations," he said. Calhoun didn't seem to have a problem dealing with Nike, however, which paid him a princely wage for a variety of duties. According to the contract, which *The Hartford Courant* obtained via the Freedom of Information Act in early 2005, Calhoun was legally bound to be a corporate bagman, to "describe to members of the team the advantages of Nike basketball shoes and other Nike products."

To be fair, Auriemma and the top women's coaches were also on the sneaker dole. Thanks to increased television coverage and the far-reaching effects of Title IX, the women's game was growing by leaps and bounds, perhaps laying the traps for its own ethical trespasses, building its own slippery slope. In the mid-1990s, I began penciling the Women's Final Four into my early April calendar. I looked forward to spending a few days with the UConns and Tennessees, with a college sport that for the time being still had strikingly sound graduation rates and at least felt like an oasis of good vibes compared to the men, whose efforts at reform were often cheap as talk.

The media's attention was always easy to divert with a few March buzzer beaters. The NCAA's 2005 decision to begin linking graduation rates to number of scholarships was called groundbreaking and historic, and even Lapchick—who not long before had told me college basketball was "so broke I'm not sure it can be fixed"—said he was hopeful "for the first time ever." The fine print, though, revealed modest goals: The minimum graduation rate was set at around 50 percent in order to avoid NCAA sanctions.

NCAA president Myles Brand deserved credit for trying, but the problem went beyond NCAA legislation. The sport suffered from a sickness deep in its soul, from a cancerous greed. Given the money at stake, the pressure to win, how could human nature be policed? How could the unscrupulous be prevented from raising the bar on creative cheating? What did a passing grade to a nonsense course mean? "I know for sure that African-American athletes are encouraged to take classes that they can't learn anything in," said Spike Lee, citing his own well-placed university sources. "Let's face it, Sports Management—that's today's equivalent of Basket Weaving."

Those classes were A.P. calculus compared to "Coaching Principles and Strategies of Basketball," taught by Jim Harrick's son and coaching assistant, Jim, Jr., at the University of Georgia. In the 2003 academic fraud fallout that cost both Harricks their jobs, the course's final exam hit the wires. Among the daunting questions: How many points does a 3-point field goal account for in a basketball game? How many halves are in a college basketball game? In what league do the Georgia Bulldogs play? This was perfectly scripted for late-night Leno, the stuff of hilarious dumb jock legend, unless you were a young African-American male, stung by the inescapable stigma of more college basketball follies, more public minstrelsy for the masses.

I can appreciate a good Senior Day cry as much as anyone, but for every college basketball player who walked out with legitimate academic credentials, at least one and in many places two or more left school with only plaques and memories. Often the argument has been made that any time spent in college was better than none, even if, as Harry Edwards agreed, "eighty percent of it was in the athletic environment." However, it seemed to me a dangerous social stereotype to celebrate those who chose to use college as their developmental highway as more virtuous than those who didn't. "I was in New York when LeBron James was coming out of high school and was listening to WFAN in the car one day," Duke professor Neal said, referring to New York's sports talk station. "These guys are screaming that LeBron should go to college for a year or two because that would make him 'a better person.' And I'm thinking, a better person? Why does the young African-American basketball player have to go to college to become 'a better person' and the white tennis player doesn't?"

It was also fair to ask what long-term career benefits were accrued from the unseemly recruiting process, from being pampered as campus king, from being insulated inside The Program? What lessons had Chris Webber absorbed at Michigan, where he received cash handouts from a shady booster? What had the practice-averse Allen Iverson learned about preparation and team play at Georgetown? What did Ron Artest know about self-restraint after two years under Mike Jarvis at St. John's? The anecdotal evidence from the mid-1990s on, post-Garnett, right on through to LeBron James, indicated that a year or two of college did not necessarily mold a better NBA citizen, or a more well-rounded person. "Give me a choice between Stephon Marbury after one year at Georgia Tech and Sebastian Telfair straight from high school, and I'll take the kid who hasn't been given free run of a major college program," one NBA executive told me.

Decades of conditioning weren't easy to get past, though. Len Elmore, an old NBA friend, the ESPN college analyst and Harvard Law grad, frowned when I first pitched an NBA minor-league alternative that would accept high-school graduates. "I just want to see as many kids in school as possible, period," he said.

Peter Roby said he feared "throwing out the baby with the bath-water," and pointed out that some very famous NBA players—Central Arkansas's Scottie Pippen, for one—had come from smaller, less-rigorous schools. Donnie Walsh of the Indiana Pacers, who had drafted players out of high school as well as trading for Jermaine O'Neal, told me he preferred that kids go to college, though he admitted, "The high-school kids have been great to deal with and every time I start to talk about this I give myself a headache."

Trying to create a one-size-fits-all formula for human beings is always migraine-inducing. The trick is getting people in power to admit that they can't solve society's ills through sports, especially when their self-interests inherently conflict with their professed ideals. In winter 2004, I was preparing a column on Maurice Clarett's ill-fated legal challenge to the NFL policy of refusing to admit players who hadn't completed their junior year of college. By sheer luck, Myles Brand, the NCAA president, was scheduled to visit the *Times* that afternoon for a sit-down with editors and reporters. Arranging to be piped in on speakerphone, I asked Brand how he countenanced the different approaches—attitudinally and otherwise—for basketball and baseball players. His answer was refreshingly reform-minded: "In basketball, in particular, the integrity of the student-athlete mission has been compromised by the proverbial pounding of the square peg into the round hole," Brand said. "Baseball has it absolutely right."

Brand said he had, in fact, just written an op-ed piece for *The Sporting News* on this very subject, arguing that college basketball could do without the Marburys, the Carmelos, the one-year wonders. There would always be kids choosing to entertain the campus hordes over toiling in minor-league America, families pushing their sons toward an education. "College sports will continue to feed its graduating athletes to professional sports," Brand said. "It always has, always will. But there should be alternatives to athletes who have little or no interest in a college education to develop themselves as professional prospects."

Square peg into round hole—a cliché born of painful truth,

the perfect accounting of the self-serving lengths people would sink to in order to force-fit and exploit young men for personal gain. College basketball was never meant to be a professional breeding ground, and didn't have to be to retain its single-elimination March splendor. With its built-in fan base, its distinct look in the days before the shot clock, the sport wove itself into the American sports fabric when most NBA franchises, including Red Auerbach's Celtics, couldn't make a nickel.

After the wildest 2005 Sweet Sixteen and Elite Eight weekend anyone could remember, I ran into Jay Price, a former colleague from my youthful days working at the *Staten Island Advance* and one of my first mentors in the business. We got to talking about what made those games so wonderfully dramatic, so memorable, and agreed that the most compelling characters of the NCAA tournament were those who in all likelihood weren't going to the next level, whose common-man, sports-fantasy stories resonated in the way conventional Olympic tales did, because the odds were that no one would ever tell them again. "You know what?" Jay said. "You could take the top one hundred kids every year, put them in the pros, and whatever kids were left, North Carolina against Duke would still be worth watching."

As soundly demonstrated by the 2005 tournament, the natural appeal of the college game was rooted in intense competition, not necessarily its caliber of play. Pleasing the critics was ultimately the mission for those claiming to be the world's best. That was David Stern's responsibility, not Myles Brand's. As the nineties unfolded, as more high-school seniors followed Kevin Garnett's lead, as basketball on all levels became more about receiving one's props than learning its precepts, the commissioner's job didn't get any easier.

7

1998: Beyond Jordan

ON THE NIGHT of Michael Jordan's last home game as a member of the Bulls, many came early to worship the mythology as much as they did the man. Ninety minutes before game five of the 1998 NBA Finals, the statue stood so tall, so proud, as the guardian of the United Center, as the bronze messiah of professional sports. Fathers with cameras dangling from their necks dispatched their children to pose by the shrine. Fans who had walked past it countless times without stopping to read the inscription now mouthed the words: "The best there ever was. The greatest there ever will be." On a pleasant June evening, pen in hand, my reporter's notebook out, I sampled the gathering crowd, and breathed in its belief that the night would be unforgettable.

Among their numbers were: a longtime season ticket holder who customarily shared two seats with friends but decided to bring his young son just so the boy could someday tell his own child, or grandchild, that he was there for Jordan's last game; a young man from familiar territory, Staten Island, engaged to be married that summer, whose brother had scored the most treasured of gifts, two in the rafters, for the presumed clincher against the Utah Jazz; a couple in from Los Angeles, self-described Jordan fanatics, carting an infant and a toddler, praying the little ones would cooperate by sleeping through the bedlam; and many others who had fought their way through Friday rush-hour traffic, without a ticket, without hope or the small fortune necessary to score one, just wanting to be near the building, around the statue, in Jordan's air space.

They all had followed the saga of championship number six, the last running of the Bulls, as orchestrated by Phil Jackson, who believed that in the completion of a second three-peat would come a sense of symmetry, an understanding that the time had come for everyone to move on. Time for the increasingly restless Jackson to take a sabbatical from the sport . . . for the cessation of hostilities between the front office and the team's core players . . . for Dennis Rodman to take his disruptive freak show someplace else . . . for David Stern to start hoping that another ratings-friendly superstar could step up, or grow up, and triumphantly carry the exceedingly Jordan-centric NBA into the twenty-first century.

Jordan and the Bulls were a global phenomenon, a television monolith, the sports equivalent of the ensemble sitcom smash. The 1998 Finals' overall Nielsen rating, 18.7, was the largest in NBA history, more than double what Magic Johnson's first championship scored in 1980, triple what the San Antonio Spurs and New Jersey Nets would record five years later. By early 1998, Jordan *was Seinfeld,* the runaway hit that also happened to be in its last season of original episodes on NBC. This network-crushing coincidence provided the muse for a whimsical column that I had more fun writing than any other I can recall: a fictitious chance meeting between the two famously eccentric casts in the Hollywood office of NBC honcho Don Ohlmeyer, who had summoned the team from *Michael* for a meeting to discuss the possibility of replacing *Seinfeld* in the Thursday night nine o'clock slot. Jerry had Kramer, George, and Elaine. Michael had Scottie, Rodman, and Phil. Jerry had Newman to deride. Michael had the body double, Jerry Krause. Like Jerry, Michael got all the love. Like George, Scottie got no respect.

In terms of pure performance, never had such a deserving second star been so lost in a teammate's luminescence, acknowledged for his skills but so underplayed on the marquee. In the series against the Jazz, a rematch of the six-game series won by the Bulls the previous year, Pippen's divide-and-conquer aggression against the kings of pick-and-roll, Utah's John Stockton and Karl Malone, was the most celebrated component of the series through five games. Not one to give gratuitous praise, even Malone had taken a moment to say that Pippen "may be the best defensive player ever." All Pippen needed in game five was another well-rounded performance in which he filled the box score with rebounds, assists, steals, and 15 or 20 points, just enough to resonate with the panel of MVP voters. "That would be very good for my free-agency résumé," Pippen volunteered in advance. Giving away his relocation plans, he spoke too soon. So close to the recognition he desired and deserved, Pippen's opportunity to upstage Jordan evaporated in the span of 48 nightmarish shooting minutes.

To his credit, he never used the excuse of back spasms he was experiencing to explain 14 of 16 missed shots, his inability to knock down open jumpers, or take advantage of post-ups against the smaller Jeff Hornacek. Had Pippen made just two more shots to go with his 11 assists, his 11 rebounds, the last championship would have been celebrated on the United Center floor. He would have had the strongest case for MVP. Instead, Malone led the Jazz to an 83–81 lead with 1.1 seconds remaining. The Bulls inbounded the ball to Jordan on the right side, behind the 3-point line, in front of the Bulls' bench. Had it all been a setup, more Nike marketing in the making? "Everybody was anticipating a big shot on our side, holding their breath," Jordan said.

Off one foot, Jordan launched an ugly air ball. This would not be the night for Bulls' fans to dance or do damage in the streets of Chicago. Exhaling, the crowd filed out solemnly onto West Madison Street. The series was going back to Utah, where Jordan—thirty-five years old, no longer a frequent flier, worn down by the long playoff grind—would be facing the championship challenge before a hostile crowd that smelled blood. Listening to Jordan that night in the interview room, seeing a familiar twinkle in his eyes, I got the sense he almost preferred the stiffer challenge, the Jazz calling him out, the media contemplating his fall. Maybe that was what separated him from other great players, the gambler inside who relished the raising of the stakes.

The next morning, before flying to Salt Lake City, I wrote my column for the Sunday *Times,* beginning with the photo-snapping statue scene before game five, ending with the air ball and a reminder that the man was infinitely more interesting than the myth: "Jordan said he often relives 1993, Game 6 in Phoenix, his send-off to a 17-month sabbatical. The Bulls were losing by 2 on their last possession. The ball, in-bounded in the backcourt, touched every player's hands before John Paxson launched a title-clinching 3, dispelling the doubt and eliminating the fear that a statue could never reflect. If this is Jordan's last season, then to see him in Utah is going to be one last, special treat. Dealing with doubt. Facing the fear. A photo opportunity, if ever there was one."

There was no doubt during the Bulls' second three-peat years and especially by the 1998 Finals that the NBA was more tethered to Jordan than ever, more responsive to his every whim, breathlessly awaiting his every word. Would Michael play for a coach other than Jackson? Would he consider returning without Scottie? Would he put up with another year of Dennis? Was this really the end?

On the subject of Jordan's eventual departure, David Stern always liked to say the sun would come up, his teams would go to training camp, the season would be played, tickets would be sold, televisions would be watched. "It's like the questions we used to be asked about if we would be concerned if a Utah made it to the Finals," Stern said, referring to the league's most remote market. "The answer is no." Stern had no difficulty tackling his rhetorical question, but the followup was more of a brain teaser: How big an attraction would the NBA Finals be when Jordan was gone, practicing his putts on a faraway green, and Utah was playing Atlanta in prime time?

Stern's contention was that the Finals had become an event that stood on its own, like the World Series or the Final Four, but the wildly fluctuating television ratings didn't support his argument, and neither did Steve Kerr. "You saw what happened when Michael retired the first time," said the Bulls' reserve guard, who had replaced John Paxson as the spot-up shooter and even hit a title-clinching jumper in 1997 against the Jazz off a pass from the double-teamed Jordan. "The ratings went way down when the Knicks played Houston, and everyone ridiculed the style of play."

From the time of Jordan's return, he and the Bulls ameliorated the pervasive sense that the NBA and American basketball as a whole were devolving. The game was becoming less about grace and skill, more about bump and grind. Chuck Daly's bad-boy Pistons in Detroit were largely credited, or blamed, for adding belligerence to grit, but it was Pat Riley who made a science out of slop art. A scrappy kid from a working-class family in upstate New York, Riley took on the trappings of a Hollywood glamor boy coaching the Lakers, but he was really a wolf in Armani clothing. He was all about rolling up the sleeves, motivating his players to play a brutally defensive game, pushing them to the emotional edge.

Amateur psychologists in the press box, myself included, couldn't help but wonder if the 1990s for Riley were in part about disproving the hackneyed belief that four Lakers championships were simply pure Magic, all about talent. They weren't, any more than the Bulls' six were exclusively about Jordan. In New York and later Miami, Riley built two Eastern Conference powers that made Daly's Pistons look like the old Boston Celtics. These teams were infused with Riley's blue-collar principles, trained under his thumb, drilled to surrender no layups or dunks without administering physical pain. Playoff series became ideological and low-scoring wars of attrition, especially following Riley's departure from New York for more power and money in Miami that left a lingering bitterness and his disciple, Jeff Van Gundy, the head man on the Knicks' bench.

Knicks-Heat series were ugly scrums, with football metaphors and fists flying, one hard foul provoking another, bench-clearing brawls begetting suspensions and widespread scorn. One typically combustible playoff night at Madison Square Garden, I was sitting within earshot of the Miami bench, when the Knicks' Latrell Sprewell hammered Terry Porter to the floor on the fast break near the conclusion of a Miami win. One of Riley's assistant coaches jumped up and started ranting to the Heat subs, "Remember all that. Remember what they do." It was Stan Van Gundy, brother of Jeff.

New York was transfixed by the intensity of the rivalry, but purists winced at what they saw, and the upshot was that neither team ever made it past Jordan into the Finals, much less won a championship. Perhaps the Bulls' greatest 1990s accomplishment was to have saved the league from being lost to the clutches of Rileyball, a point I raised in a column during the 1998 playoffs, urging Stern to legislate elegance back into the sport before it turned into professional wrestling. At a subsequent game, I was chatting with a league publicist, who said Stern had cited the column at a staff meeting, agreeing that something had to be done to rein in the physicality. I took it as a compliment, especially since Stern at the time wasn't taking my calls, the result of a book I'd co-authored with Armen Keteyian that had challenged so-called NBA investigations into the gambling escapades of Jordan and Isiah Thomas, and argued that the league was becoming too dependent on its increasingly independent stars.

For columnists like myself, Riley was a fair but occasionally too convenient target, easy to ridicule for his combative lexicon, for the way he maintained his sartorial splendor and his perfectly moussed coiffure while hell was breaking loose all around. Even Phil Jackson, who found control-freak coaches like Riley fairly repellent, admitted the contrasts were necessary, good for the game, as long as his tactics proved superior. At least Riley's teams were unified and competitive, not mere superstar showcases. He was the ruggedly handsome face of basketball's brawny bunch, but, in the larger sense, he was just a representation of a seismic shift that was occurring in the mainstream sports culture: the decline of subtlety as a popular means of athletic expression in the emerging era of performance enhancement.

Across the board, power was becoming the rage. In baseball, it was the home-run spectacle that led the majors into the depths of steroid shame. In football, it was smashmouth offenses behind linemen so bloated they resembled grounded blimps. In tennis and golf, it was bulked-up equipment that allowed players to drive balls to sport-altering distances and speeds. Basketball signed on to this model of muscle over mind with an all-out devotion and promotion of the slam dunk, and nowhere was it more corrosive than in the marketing of the player who was bigger than everyone and quickly grew second in stature to Jordan.

Back in the early eighties, during my first years covering the game, a young mountain of a man named Darryl Dawkins earned a measure of one-trick celebrity by slamming the ball with such ferocity that the backboard apparatus collapsed. Dawkins, a Philadelphia 76er during the Julius Erving days, composed names for the dunks that celebrated worthless feats of strength that sent glass shards flying and arena officials scrambling. By the nineties, Dawkins' mischievous rhymes were Shaquille O'Neal's mainstream rap, especially after Shaq broke two backboards as a rookie during the 1992–93 season. He cut an album on which he bragged, "I jam it, I slam it, I make sure it's broke."

O'Neal, seven-one, about 330 pounds of pure muscle and spellbinding quickness for a man his size, happened to be a playful kid with an engaging smile, who didn't need to glorify acts of destruction to elevate his Q score. With Jordan on his seventeen-month sabbatical, O'Neal narrowly lost out on the 1993–94 scoring title to San Antonio's David Robinson, led the league in field-goal percentage, was second in rebounding to Dennis Rodman, and lifted a fifth-year expansion team to fifty wins and its first playoff berth. He was eminently coachable, willing to share the ball, working hard on his passing skills out of the post, but the push was on to market basketball as a three-ring circus, as eye candy. This became apparent to me when I flew to London to cover the 1995 McDonald's Open, an appropriate title for the total, introductory NBA experience. Included were a woolly mascot swinging from the rafters, a ref on stilts, trampoline dunkers, a woman spinning six basketballs at once, and, for the more competitively inclined, a ring-toss exhibition featuring the moving target of a bald man with a toilet plunger affixed to his head. The British press, with its Spartan soccer sensibilities, was understandably appalled.

O'Neal, the most dominant physical presence since Wilt, was sadly packaged as a circus act, a one-man wrecking crew, more Godzilla than Barney, a monster that devastated backboards, not opposing defenses. In a soft-drink commercial, O'Neal bent a rim. In a spot for Reebok, he confounded backboard architects by smashing their supposedly unbreakable product to smithereens. Still in his early twenties, it was unreasonable to expect O'Neal to complain or grasp the enormous influence of these visuals worldwide. When his stepfather, Phillip Harrison, got into the act, shattering the glass in a phone booth after slamming the receiver while pitching for a long-distance service, we were reminded that players weren't marketing themselves. They weren't perpetrating the march that made a mockery of sport.

O'Neal's agent, Leonard Armato, said I was missing the point of the advertising campaign when I asked him what it was. He compared O'Neal's backboard busting to a tactic psychologists use when they advise clients to let off stress by beating their pillow. "A new-age thinking," Armato said. "Don't blow up a building; take it out on a rim." All around the country, teenagers were doing just that, trying to bend steal with their bare hands, leaving rimless playgrounds everywhere. A few days after my column ran, I got a call from Phil Mushnick, the *New York Post* columnist and the country's most impassioned critic of a sports culture he disdainfully considers odious and exploitive. Phil, a childhood friend of mine from Staten Island who had helped me land a job as a night clerk on the *Post* sports desk, had been my muse for the O'Neal piece after including an item in his column about a foundation whose purpose was to repair rimless backboards in New York City playgrounds. Now he was saying he'd been tipped on a story that was so upsetting, he just had to tell me—a competitor—about it before it hit the stands: A middle-school boy in upstate New York had died after hanging and falling from a rim. The kid was buried with the jersey of his favorite player, Shaquille O'Neal.

For the record, the NBA said it didn't approve of such marketing mindlessness, but it continued to put its licensing stamp on video games that included backboard-breaking jams and other socially repugnant features. These new revenue streams blinded Stern and other executives as to how perceptions of their game were changing, how fundamentals and team play were no longer the primary outtake for a generation of kids watching slam-dunk highlights on ESPN. Power begot prestige and prestige meant you got paid. O'Neal, for his part, soon reeled in $121 million for relocating, for spurning flat, humid, and landlocked Orlando for Southern California's beachfront properties. No one could argue he wasn't the worth the money or that it was a bad career move, but the timing of the 1996 announcement that he had signed with the Lakers amounted to another basketball spectacle.

"I'm a military child, used to moving every three or four years," O'Neal explained at the press conference to announce the free-agent signing. "Change is good." So is greed, Michael Douglas once argued as Gordon Gekko in the movie *Wall Street*, but O'Neal insisted that the $121 million Orlando couldn't afford to retain him was not the reason he had signed with Los Angeles. "I'm tired of hearing about money, money, money, money," he said, in his playful way. "I just want to play the game, drink Pepsi, wear Reebok." In a setting more conducive to the economic excesses of professional sports, such clever doublespeak would have been good for a laugh. But, as if staging the O'Neal press confer-

ence on the eve of the Summer Olympics wasn't bad enough tim-
ing, consider the league's taste: The O'Neal press conference was
held the day after TWA Flight 800 exploded after takeoff from
New York's Kennedy Airport and crashed off Long Island, killing
all 229 aboard, leaving the country shocked by what was feared
to be a terrorist act.

Despite a Dream Team roster stocked with veterans of
Barcelona (Pippen, Malone, Stockton, David Robinson) in an obvious response to the debacle in Toronto, American basketball
was once again cast as grossly commercial, unflinchingly crass. At
the '96 Atlanta Olympic Games, preoccupied with the emerging
women's movement in basketball, soccer, and softball, I barely
paid attention as the Americans trounced the opposition by an average of 34.5 points, winning seven straight games. The hero worship we saw in Barcelona was gone, however. The novelty of the
Dream Team had worn off. Only Jordan, who had elected not to
play, seemed to have the golden touch. Only he was capable of
keeping critics from carping about the qualitative deterioration of
the NBA game.

Defenses were more sophisticated, more aggressive, than
they'd been throughout the eighties but, as Oscar Robertson
wrote in a 2004 op-ed piece for *The New York Times,* "When
people tell me the scores are lower today because defenses are better, I have to laugh. Players are bigger, faster, stronger and more
agile, but many of them can't dribble, can't shoot from outside,
can't create off the dribble." Offenses were stagnant with less
movement of body and ball, with isolations and two-man games,
and an alarming number of role players instructed to rebound,
block shots, and stay out of the way on the offensive end. Another
legend, Magic Johnson, chimed in, lamenting how "The whole
game became taking your man off the dribble, crossing over,
dunking on him or shooting a three."

Arguably the most flamboyant fundamentalist in history,
Magic years later offered his opinion on the decline of the game
beginning in the mid-1990s, why it was no longer cool to play

below the rim, stay on one's feet, make a simple bounce pass. Why had it become no longer fashionable to be Magic? "It's funny," he said, "when Larry and I came into the league, it was right after the ABA brought all the great one-on-one players and everyone said, 'Wow, Magic and Larry, they aren't that fast, they can't jump, but they play such a fundamentally sound game, they make everyone better, and people loved it. But in the last ten years, all of a sudden it was a lot of one on one. Everybody wanted to dunk like Michael but what they didn't realize was that what made Michael great was his knowledge of the fundamentals. Individual play was back in the NBA, and that made it come back in the college game and that made it come back in high school. Dunks and threes, dunks and threes, and kids weren't working on anything in between."

The gradual breakdown across the 1990s of fundamental basketball skills was startling, as was the statistical evidence in the pro game. By the 1997–98 season, only four teams averaged 100 points or more, Shaq's Lakers topping out at 105.5, as opposed to a decade earlier, when all but one team averaged 100 or more and nine exceeded 110. In 1997–98, twelve teams made less than 45 percent of their shots. In 1987–88, none did. In 1987–88, even Daly's Pistons averaged 101 points while losing the seven-game Finals to Pat Riley's Lakers. Ten years later, Jordan and the Bulls averaged 88 points in the six games against Utah, not much better than the much-decried 86-point average Houston scratched out against the Knicks in '94.

Predictably enough, there was no outcry during or after the Bulls-Jazz series regarding the depths to which the offenses had fallen, even after the Jazz bottomed out with a record-low 54 points in game three. Not with Jordan still around, all eyes upon him as he sneaked up behind Karl Malone on the baseline, stole the ball in the waning seconds of game six, the Bulls trailing by a point. As Jordan dribbled past midcourt at the Delta Center that night, more television viewers of any basketball game in history contemplated the perfect symmetry, the closure of the circle. Pippen was crippled by back pain, of little help that night. Toni

Kukoc was still not worthy of Jordan's trust, not on an occasion such as this one. Stockton knew enough not to leave Steve Kerr to double-team Jordan after Kerr had burned the Jazz the previous spring. Jordan was flying solo, the end of his Bulls' career looking suspiciously like the beginning. In his last game for the Bulls, he took 35 shots, scored 45 points in forty-four minutes, including their last 8, and the most celebrated basket of the modern NBA, the pull-up, midrange jumper that was once a fundamental basketball staple but had almost gone the way of the two-hand set.

The younger Jordan would have just levitated over the Jazz defender, Bryon Russell, but the thirty-five-year-old, more earthbound version needed all the tricks of the trade to clear enough space. "I made my initial drive, he bit, I stopped, pulled up, great look," Jordan explained. He conveniently managed to edit out his use of the left shoulder and arm, and the belief of many that in a true basketball meritocracy, he would have been called for pushing off the defender. Years later, I had the opportunity to ask Russell about the play that punctuated Jordan's six-championship legend, when he was a teammate of Malone's with Phil Jackson's Lakers, in the 2004 Finals against Detroit. As I roamed the court at The Palace of Auburn Hills, gathering quotes for a tribute column on the injured Malone and his doomed quest for a championship ring, I spotted Russell sitting by himself in the stands. I asked him if he and Malone had ever talked about the Jordan jumper in Salt Lake, if after all the years and replays he wished he could go back and try it again.

He shook his head, ruefully. "I've had referees come up to me and say they would have made that call, but who was going to call a push-off at that time on the greatest player to ever play the game?" Russell said. "That night, it just felt like they weren't going to let us win." He wasn't crying fix, only asserting that sentimentality played a role. The refs willed the Hollywood ending they intuitively knew the world wanted to see and maybe they did as well. The replay also revealed, at least from the way I saw it, that as Jordan began his dribble drive, Russell reached for the ball, got too close, drawing unnecessary contact, and committing the cardinal defensive sin of not staying balanced, feet uncrossed. That was exactly the mistake Russell had made in game one of the previous year's Finals, when Jordan took the bump and countered with a buzzer-beater from the left wing to win the game. Once again, by the time Jordan was in the air, the ball released, his right hand bent in a signature message to the world that he knew exactly where it was going, Russell may as well have been up in the rafters, sitting next to me in the auxiliary press area.

When the ball settled in the net with 5.2 seconds remaining, when the arena sounded just like America West in Phoenix five years before, dead silent, those of us who had chronicled the Jordan/Bulls championship years surrendered our journalistic visage, our neutral veneer. Even if you believed that Jordan got away with a nudge, these calls could be argued to eternity and in this new era of chronic inaccuracy, there was only one way to record it for posterity: Jordan made the damn shot.

In a classic *ESPN The Magazine* photo, the expressions on the faces of the fans behind the basket told the story: looks of horror on most, but smirks of grudging acknowledgment festooning others. They knew the son of a gun had ice in his veins and he was not going to blow the ultimate fantasy for a departing sports legend. And I, who still believed the deification was too often overdone, could only shake my head, watch in awe with a goofy grin as Jordan pranced about, six fingers raised high. With deadline looming, the fairy tale had to be recounted in roughly thirty minutes. Before typing my lead, I sacrificed two or three to place a telephone call to the little Bulls' fan back home in his Jordan jersey, allowed up past his bedtime. The game had started a few minutes past seven thirty in the East, making it one of the last NBA Finals game to end long before midnight, as the NBA, like most other corporate sports entities, surrendered more of its soul to satisfy network time-slotting and salvage an extra Nielsen rating point. It was Sunday night, about ten when I called home, having just witnessed a basketball moment for the ages. Like the father with his young son at the statue in Chicago, I just wanted to share it.

The qualitative decline of basketball in America was in full view by 1998, but sometimes in life there are distinct and symbolic moments when opinion becomes widely accepted as fact. In the case of the NBA, it happened in one season, in one evening, and with one shot. Jordan's end-game heroics in Salt Lake City had barely lost its buzz when the league was shut down in a near-calamitous seven-month lockout that did not conclude until February 1999, and was followed by the long-anticipated breakup of the Bulls' dynasty. Jordan retired for a second time, Pippen was traded to Houston, and Jackson took a one-year sabbatical before hooking up with Shaquille and Kobe Bryant in Los Angeles.

Stern called the lockout "a battle over two billion dollars," while much of the public called the players selfish. The response was predictable, although the union leaders, Patrick Ewing and Alonzo Mourning, hadn't exactly engendered sympathy by fumbling the issues like so many bounce passes into the post. They conceded that they made a lot of money by any societal standard, but the public needed to consider their lifestyles. They scheduled cheesy fundraisers in gambling venues and said they'd rather lose the season than compromise on the issues. Ewing urged they boycott the 1998 World Championships in Greece rather than let the NBA marketing wing cash in, but soon after was heard broadcasting a WNBA game for the Knicks parent company. While Stern and Billy Hunter dished out their propaganda, not once did I ever hear anyone on either side express concern about maintaining some semblance of affordability for the blue-collar fan.

One public-relations disaster after another made me wonder where the union leaders of old—savvy point guards such as its founder, Bob Cousy, or Oscar Robertson and Isiah Thomas—had gone. "That's why we're in this situation," Charles Oakley,

Ewing's ornery Knicks teammate who was losing millions during a balloon contract season, the haul of his life, said when I called to ask how he was coping. He linked the players' labor problems to their on-court woes. "You have all these so-called franchise players who aren't leaders, who don't make anyone better."

When the lockout ended and a fifty-game schedule was hastily arranged, Jordan let the NBA know he wouldn't be around to win back the fans. As Stern predicted, the sun came up, the season commenced, but as the critics expected, ratings for the '99 Finals between the Knicks and the Spurs sank like a basketball made of stone, from 18.7 plus to 11.3. It began to set in that there would be no more rating bonanzas without Jordan, without a player consistently capable of blurring between reality and myth. It was instructive to remember that the Jordan era had flourished over years, as had Magic's and Bird's. The NBA would have been wise to focus on repairing the game, promoting team play. In fast-food, hard-sell, and quick-fix America, however, it was too tempting to wag the dog, stick a budding star in the microwave, and set the dial to Next Jordan. Especially when Vince Carter came along, drafted by Toronto at the very time Jordan quit the Bulls.

Was it luck, fate, an act of the Nike gods? Like Jordan, Carter had played three years at North Carolina . . . he was six-six . . . a magician in the air, an artistic dunker who seemed, free of Dean Smith's constraints, ready to take over the airwaves. By his second season, Carter was Vinsanity . . . Half Man, Half Amazing . . . Air Canada. He was the new pro-basketball poster boy, the network go-to guy. "I think it was a mistake," Magic Johnson said. "Michael was Michael, but what happened with Vince was that we stopped promoting teams that were winners, and we went with individuals. It wasn't the Boston Celtics with Larry Bird and Kevin McHale against the Lakers with Magic and Kareem anymore. It wasn't the Pistons and the Bulls or even the Knicks and Miami. Now it was Vince Carter against Allen Iverson. And it was always the individuals that could make the crowd yell for one play, not the players like Tim Duncan, Jason Kidd, the guys that made everyone better, who understood the team game. That's what we lost."

Stern argued that the media was the primary culprit in the overpromotion of young players, insisting that no one in the NBA, least of all him, had a mandated preference for players hanging spectacularly from the rim, as opposed to the likes of Duncan, whose sturdy shoulders held up his team. Television was the engine driving the product, however, and Stern was always intimately involved in the league's TV packages, in how the league was presented. Week after week, the tunnel vision was all too apparent in the case of Carter, especially on the night Duncan and the defending champion Spurs visited Madison Square Garden in March 2000 for a rematch of the previous spring's Finals, which the Knicks had played without the injured Ewing.

Now Ewing was healthy, creating an intriguing what-if scenario, while Duncan, in only his third season, was already the reigning Finals' MVP who had wasted glamor guy Shaq and the Lakers 4–0 in the Western Conference semis. He was that rare young franchise player who cared little about his stats or the size of his rival's shoe deal. The most diversely skilled low-post player since Bill Walton—who, when young and healthy, was the best I ever saw—Duncan became a favorite from the first time I watched him loft out-of-vogue bank shots as a Wake Forest junior one wintry night at Maryland's old Cole Fieldhouse.

Len Elmore, then trying to make a living as a player-agent, was sitting in the seat next to me. "This kid is the whole package," Elmore said. Duncan was also an academic throwback, choosing to graduate from Wake, to fulfill a promise he made to his mother when she was dying of cancer in St. Croix, the Virgin Islands. Most basketball people believed Duncan's fundamental purity— his footwork on the low post was impeccable and he almost never dribbled unnecessarily or brought the ball below shoulder level, where it could be stripped away—had more to do with being a latecomer to the sport, unexposed to the look-at-me AAU meat market.

Subtlety was a hard sell, be it in the run for the NBA championship or the twenty-first century White House. The previous spring, Duncan and the Spurs had flunked the Jordan-standard ratings test, and disappointing Mr. Nielsen meant automatic banishment to a purgatory for the criminally mundane. TNT showed the Knicks-Spurs game to only half the country, while Carter, who had yet to appear in a playoff game, was being force-fed again to the other half. Once again, the message was clear: The team game, the core product, wasn't sexy enough to stand on its own. A beautifully well-rounded player like Duncan, who came to be known as The Big Fundamental, was considered too dull.

None of this was Carter's fault. He didn't ask to be Jordan. Dean Smith had warned him before he left Chapel Hill not to fall into that trap. "I never wanted that to happen," Carter said. "Michael Jordan was who he was, and he obviously had the time to create the legend. I was just a young guy trying to come in and get his feet wet and enjoy the life of an NBA player. I might have had flashes of Michael, but I said from the beginning that I wasn't Michael Jordan. I didn't want that pressure. Nobody listened."

Sitting in the practice gym after being traded to New Jersey during the 2004–05 season, Carter was ecstatic to be anywhere but Toronto, where, over the years, as injuries and losses mounted, he became a sullen, malingering presence, believing he had been set up to fail, at one point becoming so disenchanted he threatened to stop dunking altogether. He was right about the fact that he had been set up by insufferable and shortsighted marketing. The NBA committed an act of self-sabotage that was obvious to me before Carter and Tracy McGrady led the Raptors to their playoff debut against the Knicks in April 2000.

Drafted one year before Carter out of high school, McGrady had languished on the bench for most of two years, growing into his lanky body, and was just scratching the surface of his immense talent at the perfect time, the end of his contractual commitment to Toronto. He and Carter had the potential to become an explosive NBA twosome, but I told Carter I knew their association was doomed when the NBA hype began for him and predicted as much before they lost to the Knicks in the first round. "How did you know that?" Carter asked. I told him it was simply a case of understanding the modern basketball mind. When he had been anointed the next Jordan, it meant McGrady could only be . . .

Carter nodded knowingly and cut me off, as if we were playing word association. "Pippen," he said, the obvious inference being that no NBA star worth his shoe deal could accept such one-sided casting. Remarkable as it was that McGrady, a player three years removed from high school, would consider being The Next Pippen as more curse than compliment, this was as clear a case of the myopia afflicting young basketball stars by the turn of the century. Unless you had your own team, ruled like Jordan, you were nobody. "Tracy wanted to be The Guy, not The Other Guy, and people were always referring to Toronto as my team," Carter said. "I see Tracy now, he's become T-Mac, and I think about what could have been, how we could have had something special."

Even as he counted his blessings to be out of Toronto, tearing up the league alongside assist-happy Jason Kidd as the Nets made a late run into the 2004–05 playoffs, Carter was not the only one with career misgivings. Stephon Marbury cried when he landed with best-buddy Kevin Garnett in Minneapolis on draft night in 1996 but blew town two years later with a clear case of contract envy, and hasn't had a teammate that good since. During a three-title ride, Kobe Bryant never counted his big-man blessings, never stopped plotting to escape Shaq's shadow. When he finally did, when the Lakers accommodated his power lust by shipping Shaq to Miami, Kobe learned the hard lessons of being left on his own, along a fault line.

"What's happened is that guys lost touch with the reason why you play, to win," Magic Johnson said. "They want that power but the power comes with the responsibility. What they don't realize is that if great players can't learn how to play together, then they can't be great because they can't win." By the turn of the century, that lesson for the contemporary NBA star was about to be learned on yet another stage. It was time for the next global showcase, the 2000 Olympics, when America's best basketball players woke up to a fast-changing world, and realized it was no bad dream.

8

2000: Sydney

IF THE MAJORITY of NBA players were coming to grips with a stream of European players by the turn of the century, they surely were not conceptually prepared for Yao Ming, for a future number-one draft pick from mainland China who stood seven feet five inches tall. Who raised, for American protectionists, a most disturbing question. Was there any place left on earth where very tall, athletic men could not acquire the skills necessary to play in the world's best basketball league and didn't pose a long-term threat to the U.S. stranglehold on the sport? Perhaps the Arctic, but the unmistakable evidence that the basketball world had forever changed was the vertically breathtaking vision of Yao bracing himself for Vince Carter's aerial assault and turning the lane into a Chinese no-fly zone. The moment he summarily rejected Carter's attempt to launch the 2000 Sydney Summer Olympics with a signature slam, the alarm rang for American basketball aficionados to pay much closer attention to the global changes, to rise above our cultural ignorance, find out which was the surname and the given name.

Was it Yao Ming or Ming Yao? Several newspapers initially got it wrong, but equally uninformed were the U.S. Olympic team scouting reports. "We were told that the big kid, Yao, was like Shawn Bradley," recalled Larry Brown, who served as an assistant to Rudy Tomjanovich for the NBA's third Olympic expedition. Bradley, seven-six, was the second pick out of Brigham Young of the 1993 draft but, after flashes of athletic promise, had turned out to be nothing more than a timid journeyman. Just twenty years old and painfully inexperienced, Yao couldn't stay out of foul trouble against NBA-level aggression, but, for a few eye-opening minutes, he was a commanding presence, an Asian revelation, on both ends of the floor. "I'm sitting there looking at him, the way he moves, the fundamental passing and ball-handling skills that he already has, and I'm thinking that in four years, he could be one of the best players in the world," Brown said.

That was a mouthful, and another indictment of the American system, which, after Shaquille O'Neal and Alonzo Mourning, had stopped producing multidimensional centers. Now the idea of a potential Chinese star popularizing the NBA in a country as densely populated as China took the subject of globalization to a whole new level, given the assumption that Yao could shake himself free of the Communist bureaucracy. Working in his favor was that Beijing was bidding for the 2008 Summer Games, which provided me the gist of a column. Familiar with how Olympic host countries considered it an obligation of supreme national interest to move heaven and earth for the creation of home-turf medal harvests, I predicted that Yao would be playing in the NBA within a couple of years if Beijing got the Games when the IOC made its selection the following summer. Unfortunately, I didn't stop there, and went on to argue that if the cocky American basketball professionals were ever going to look up at an Olympic scoreboard that cast them as losers, "the country that is going to achieve this miracle is China."

It didn't seem far-fetched that night, because the breakup of the Soviet Union and Yugoslavia appeared to have had a demystifying effect on the European game. Most of the foreign stars of the '92 Games had passed from the scene, leaving a younger group that American sports journalists were not familiar with and, by extension, did not take seriously. That summer, Dirk Nowitzki was just beginning to crank up as a seven-foot German scoring machine in Dallas. In Sacramento, the veteran Vlade Divac was manning the middle and a young Serb forward named Peja Sto-jakovic had opened some eyes as a perimeter marksman, averaging 11 points per game during the 1999–2000 season. Before Sydney, no one would have predicted that the Olympic Games would be any different than the previous two, and that included the U.S. players. Asked after the China game if he could foresee a serious challenge, a possible defeat, on the horizon, Mourning laughed, dismissively. "It won't be in my lifetime," he said.

Shaquille O'Neal and Kobe Bryant had two months earlier won their first NBA championship in Los Angeles under Phil Jackson, but declined to play in Sydney. Tim Duncan and Grant Hill were injured. Allen Iverson and Chris Webber were shunned as behavioral risks. Anchored in the middle by Mourning, the team was still loaded with All-Star talent, with young, seasoned frontline studs such as Kevin Garnett, Antonio McDyess, and Shareef Abdur-Rahim. Carter was the resident high flier, Tim Hardaway the explosive guard. Ray Allen, Allan Houston, and Steve Smith were the spot-up shooters. Gary Payton and Jason Kidd were the best point guards in the game. Compared to what was to come in Athens four years later, the 2000 team was a carefully woven quilt.

As the score mounted during the China game, as Yao fouled out early in the second half, another series of dreadful blowouts seemed unavoidable. Some in the American basketball media section—not most—had already come to the conclusion that the NBA had overstayed its Olympic welcome. The Barcelona Games were a global lovefest, Atlanta an American pep rally. In Sydney, playing before fans known for their high standards of sportsmanship, the Dream Team was cast in a new role, Yankee pariah. It didn't help when the truculence of the Toronto team resurfaced, when Vince Carter tangled with native son Andrew Gaze in an exhibition game in Melbourne. Carter knocked Gaze down, stood over him, like Ali over Liston. Gaze was promptly chosen by the

Australian Olympic Committee to carry the country's flag at the opening ceremonies. Carter and the Dream Team thereafter were anti-Aussies, ugly Americans.

The incident underscored the no-win position the NBA stars were in. As long as they continued bashing all comers, what else was there to root for than for them to be knocked on their American badasses? "I stayed in the athletes' village from Barcelona on," Donny Nelson said, "and over the course of time, the perception of the Dream Team became something very different." Early on in Sydney, you could see how much so in the body language of the opponents. They were pushing back, shouting back, playing as if they weren't impressed. With the benefit of hindsight, why would they have been? Far from the bejeweled heroes of Barcelona, the collective number of NBA championship rings owned by the members of Dream Team III added up to zero. Long gone were Magic, Larry, Michael and all they represented. The wall of intimidation was crumbling, and with a suddenness that defied logical progression, so did the sense of monolithic American supremacy.

On the night of a memorable and historic men's basketball semifinal, the United States against Lithuania, I was in my hotel room in downtown Sydney, working on a feature story about an Israeli kayaker, who was trying on the final weekend of the Games to win his country's first medal after several achingly close fourth-place finishes by other Israelis in Sydney. The race was called a K1 sprint and while I didn't know a K1 from a canine, I couldn't argue that the story didn't have political and social heft: Michael Kolganov was an Uzbek immigrant representing a country that was at best ambivalent about imports like him. Even more compelling was the start of the intifada—the Palestinian uprising that would inflame the Middle East—that was sending shock waves through the Israeli Olympic delegation.

The story was requested from the office back in New York,

which had the good sense to know a great big Olympics was going on outside the basketball arena. I, of course, wanted to see the United States–Lithuania game, but the kayaking venue was a two-hour commute from Sydney, and my itinerary was further complicated when the races were delayed several hours by wind. There was no way for me to get to the Olympic Park and write the story at a reasonable hour before fatigue set in from my very long day. The *Times* did have a reporter at the game and, as far as a column being necessary, what were the chances of Lithuania—which had given the Dream Team its stiffest test ever in the preliminary round, trailing by 5 with 1:09 left before losing by 9—repeating what Donny Nelson, still volunteering as a Lithuanian assistant, had called a "near miracle"?

My colleague George Vecsey was also wandering about Sydney, and he and I agreed to keep our cell phones turned on in the event the unforeseen occurred. One of us would still have all night and into the next day, if an upset occurred, to rustle up a column for the Saturday paper. The time difference meant the game was being played in the wee hours of Friday morning back home, too late for that day's edition. Sure enough, the fateful call came just as I was putting the finishing touches on the Israeli story, trying to decide between a room-service dinner or passing out in my clothes after having been up since five thirty that morning. "We're losing," said Bill Brink, the *Times*'s assistant sports editor and Sydney bureau chief. "You'd better turn on the television."

Which I immediately did, only to be reminded that the Australian network showing the Games was as provincial in its coverage as our own American hype machine, NBC. While the greatest upset in the history of basketball was conceivably occurring, Australian viewers were enjoying a taped rerun of an afternoon women's field hockey match. More than a little pissed, just a wee bit panicked, I called Brink in the bureau and asked, "Where's George?" Brink said Vecsey was out, too far from the arena. Now the game was winding down near the five-minute mark, still shockingly tight, and winning or losing was not really the issue anymore. The United States couldn't shake Lithuania, couldn't impose its will. The end of dominance—that was the column that needed to be written. We decided our only course of action was to have Brink, who had every television feed available to him in the main press center, do play-by-play, his best Marv Albert.

So, that is how I covered the breathtaking and narrow escape by the Dream Team, the night the basketball world permanently adjusted its perceptions, realized the distant future was soon, if not now. Earlier in the Games, Mourning had suggested that this version of the Dream Team was the best defensive team ever assembled, but the Lithuanians exposed it with patience, with perimeter shooting the dunk-happy Americans couldn't match, with a sagging zone defense that challenged them to try. All that saved the United States was Vince Carter's running floater in the lane, a put-back basket by Antonio McDyess off a missed free throw, and most of all, two missed free throws at the 43-second mark by a Lithuanian, Ramunas Siskauskas, who in the Olympic tournament had made 16 in a row. Despite the Americans' victory, the final score—U.S.A. 85, Lithuania 83—sounded like a prank.

Energized by the story and two cups of coffee, I rushed into a taxi and made it to the arena in about forty minutes. Fortunately, there were still more than enough people around for me to work a column, beginning with Donny Nelson, who looked as if he'd seen a ghost and vowed never to coach another game against the United States. "As proud as I am of what we just did, those weren't just a bunch of NBA All-Stars out there," he said. "They had USA across their chests, a country I'd die for." As an American, Nelson also had to admit that he wasn't very proud of how the Dream Team huddled up in the center of the court, walking off without acknowledging the Lithuanians . . . of how Larry Brown snapped in the searing heat of the moment and angrily chased after the refs into the bowels of the arena as if they were to blame for what felt like comeuppance . . . of how almost immediately the excuses began to pile up like American jumpshots clanging off the rim.

The allowance of zone defenses, strange officiating, no Shaq, the shorter 3-point shot line, the lack of practice time before the Games, no Shaq, the wider lane and, did we mention, no Shaq. In eight short years, the Dream Team went from utterly invincible to lamenting the dissimilarity of the rules and the absence of a player or two, while trying to explain how it had nearly gone down to a country with a population, 3.7 million, that was smaller than Sydney's. To a team without a single player with NBA experience. Looking back on that night, Nelson said the U.S. problem wasn't who played. It was how. The years of obsessive marketing, of egomaniacal excesses, had come home to roost. "Shooting, passing, moving without the ball have become secondary to players who are more concerned with dunking like Michael Jordan and selling one-hundred-fifty-dollar shoes," Nelson said, sadly.

All around, feelings were raw, even in the media workroom. Much as we had developed an affinity for the international players, it was clear to me that Americans weren't any more prepared emotionally to deal with the sudden challenge than Canadians were when the Soviet hockey teams showed up in the 1970s and began kicking some serious NHL butt. Listening on the telephone during those tense final seconds, I can admit that I was rooting for the United States to pull the game out and I know that many of my colleagues were, too. Rooting is one thing. Reporting is another. It was time to face facts, give credit where it was due. "What we learn from them," David Stern said of the Europeans before the United States struggled again to defeat France for the gold medal, "is what they learned from us."

Beginning in Barcelona, the early tutorials administered by the Dream Team had obviously been put to good use and no one had reason to be prouder than Sarunas Marciulionis. His effort, his investment, had paid a great dividend. Marciulionis did not attend the Olympics in 2000. He watched the semifinal at home, along with everyone else in his basketball-crazed country. Five years later, when I called him in Vilnius and asked him to relive that night, emotion crept into his voice. "Before the game, I would have said this could not happen, even though by then we had started to see the U.S. teams losing in the junior tournaments," he said. "But this was still the NBA and if we had won, I would have said it was the biggest upset in basketball, ever, like the Miracle on Ice, only bigger because of how small our country is. During the second half, as it got near the end, I kept saying, 'I can't believe it, I can't believe it.' I also remember my political thought: If we could play like this against the best basketball country in the world, the government should build basketball schools because the game is putting Lithuania on the map."

I asked him if he was disappointed by the outcome, how many times in his mind he had replayed the missed free throws or the end-game 3-point heave by another Sarunas—last name of Jasikevicius—that fell short. "Of course at the moment, yes," Marciulionis said. "But everyone in Vilnius was so proud, with tears. We look back and know that game changed everything. It was a statement for European basketball, for the whole world. Everyone knew then they could play. Everyone knew they could compete." Somewhere, his Russian mentor, Alexsandr Gomelsky, was nodding in agreement.

Two years after Sydney, I enjoyed my rare prognosticative triumph when, following the selection of Beijing as the 2008 Summer Olympics city, Yao Ming was made the first pick of the 2002 NBA draft by the Houston Rockets. Much as Yao's negotiated release from the Chinese authorities resonated from West to Far East, elated as Stern and Company were to add a billion or so potential jersey buyers and television watchers to the fold, the more eye-opening aspect of the draft came soon after. With the fifth pick, Denver tabbed a kid whose name chimed with consonants but rang no bells: Nikoloz Tskitishvili, a seven-footer from that basketball hotbed, the Republic of Georgia. With the seventh pick, the Knicks baffled the hometown crowd at the Madison Square Garden draft site by landing a Brazilian power forward, Nene Hilario, only to trade him and Marcus Camby to Denver for

Antonio McDyess. That meant three of the top seven picks were from abroad, none of them from the traditional European powers. What was going on?

Clearly, the 2000 Olympics had emboldened NBA executives, as had the accelerated development of Nowitzki in Dallas and Stojakovic in Sacramento to All-Star status. By the time the New Jersey Nets, drafting twenty-fourth, picked a nineteen-year-old Serb, center Nenad Krstic, six foreign players had been anointed in the first round on the way to a record fifteen picks overall, roughly one-fourth of the entire draft. On the TNT network set, Charles Barkley had seen enough. The foreign players, he said, were gaining an advantage. "They have been playing in pro leagues since they were fifteen or sixteen." Barkley said, while American teenagers were being manipulated by the colleges and corporations for the purpose of propagating the NCAA industry, which Barkley called "a scam." Unmindful of the presence of Missouri coach Quin Snyder, he took the opportunity to indict college coaches as "crooks" who don't graduate players or teach them how to play. Snyder defensively admitted the European system of player development "may be more functional."

Embracing a Marciulionis, tolerating a Drazen Petrovic, was one thing. Now jobs were being taken. Ability and understanding of the game, *our* game, was being questioned. Inevitably, there had to be a backlash to all the talk about how American players were fundamentally deficient, inferior in that regard to foreign players. This began to sound suspiciously retrogressive to some, too much like a rationale for a different agenda: tapping into foreign markets by recruiting their home boys and, in the process, broadening the appeal in the United States by making it more of a rainbow coalition.

Several players, including a couple with strong union ties, begged anonymity when I asked about the draft but admitted the trends made them wonder if the league was attempting to, as one player put it, "get whiter." In *The New York Times,* my colleague William C. Rhoden wrote, "European influence may be on the rise but not because players in the U.S. can't hit an outside shot. There seems to be a taste for a new flavor." Calling the foreign invasion business-related, not racist, Harry Edwards nonetheless issued a warning: The NBA risked having its product, which he labeled "as black as jazz and the blues," becoming an indistinguishable hybrid of culture and style.

These underlying tensions surfaced at the rookie orientation program at a New Jersey office park hotel prior to the opening of NBA training camps in the fall of 2002. Addressing the rookies at large, TNT commentator Kenny Smith, a former point guard on two Houston Rockets championship teams, spoke directly to the American players when he warned that their jobs were increasingly at risk as the league enthusiastically mined new marketing frontiers, looking for any excuse to draft players from abroad. Recounting his speech to me, Smith said he asked the Americans, referring to the foreign players: "Are they better than you? I don't think so. Are there some who have been drafted but they're not as good as you? Who knows? But they have a perception about you." What is it? someone asked. Smith continued: "That you're lazy, you don't work hard, you're not coachable, and you're arrogant. And the perception of the foreign players is that they work hard, love to be coached." Ultimately, this us-versus-them treatise provoked Jiri Welsch of the Czech Republic to stand up and confront Smith for being disrespectful to the foreign legion.

Smith told Welsch that wasn't his intention; it was to send a message to the American players to wake up and smell the imported blends of coffee. "I started a fire, I'll tell you that much," Smith recalled. "But I wanted to let the American players know that guys are going to be taken ahead of them because of a stereotype, and as an African-American, I don't like stereotypes. I want to say on the record that I'm for the international player because—again, as an African-American—I'm for inclusion. But I think the American players have gotten a bad rap. It's become vogue to say, 'I went overseas and I found the next Nowitzki.' There's not a lot of Nowitzkis in the world. He's already here. But the general managers can save their hides if the player doesn't perform. He can say, 'It's the language barrier, the cultural barrier.' I think some of the Europeans get a free pass."

Considering Stern's insatiable zest for marketing, given the way many teams during the seventies and eighties stocked the end of their benches with white players to ensure a modicum of racial diversity, it wasn't unreasonable for Smith and others to be wary of the accelerating internationalization, wondering if it was purely dollar-driven with a residual goal of loosening the African-American hold on the league. In the years following Larry Bird's retirement, many NBA people, Bird among them, spoke freely and even appreciatively about how the league had profited by having a transcendent white superstar like himself, which I took as part vindication for the abuse Filip Bondy of the *New York Daily News* and I took for writing a book in the early 1990s arguing that the Celtics had deliberately marketed themselves as the white team in a black sport. Our critics angrily denounced us for calling Red Auerbach, the Celtics' paternal architect, a racist, which was a wholly false interpretation of the premise.

Obviously, Stern was thrilled by how the sport was evolving, following the path of the National Hockey League, with much greater visibility and prospects for profit. To suggest the motives were racially related required a leap of logic and a disregarding of fact. Whatever gains were made abroad, the home front still represented the NBA's primacy. Players named Zarko and Zydrunas were hardly locks to become popular icons in the parochial United States, where European athletes—tennis being the perfect example—were typically ignored. When Shaquille O'Neal entered the league to wild applause from the mythmakers, Nigerian-born Hakeem Olajuwon was the best center in the league, a terrifically entertaining and canny post player. At the top of his game in the mid-nineties, winning back-to-back titles in Houston, Olajuwon was a complete mystery to Madison Avenue.

In the mid-eighties, before Barcelona, Olajuwon was a harbinger of the international movement, recruited out of Lagos by

the University of Houston. Several years later came Dikembe Mu-
tombo from the former Zaire (now Congo) to patrol the paint for
John Thompson at Georgetown. While Thompson and other college coaches had no qualms assailing the NCAA for trying to limit
scholarships as punitive to the African-American community,
there was no place on earth they wouldn't go to land a quality big
man. Now, foreign players were aiming higher. Many were white.
Others streaming into the league—be it from France or Brazil—
were not. Several NBA executives and agents told me they believe
Africa is just beginning to percolate as the next gold mine of
talent.

"The game is blind and it doesn't care what religion or color
you are," said Gregg Popovich, whose 2004–05 Spurs started, in
addition to the Virgin Islands' Duncan, a French point guard
(Tony Parker), an Argentine shooting guard (Manu Ginobili),
and, until late in the season, a Slovenian center (Rasho Nes-
terovic). On his bench were another Slovenian (Beno Udrih) and a
New Zealander (Sean Marks). Argentina's Fabricio Oberto, a star
in Spain, was signed for the 2005–06 season. Kenny Smith's argument that drafting foreign players bought NBA front-office executives time was part right: The advantage to drafting young
foreigners like the Spurs' Ginobili, Utah's Andrei Kirilenko, and
New Jersey's Nenad Krstic was that they could be left to develop
on a pro team abroad and brought over when they were ready to
contribute. Without a true minor league, young, inexperienced,
and physically unprepared Americans took up valuable roster
space and drew a paycheck.

More than a stereotype, that was just common sense, another
example of how the American system was working against its
own players at a time when the competition for NBA jobs was
stiffening. "There are just too many good players from all over
now," Popovich said. I asked him if the Spurs were an anomaly or
a representation of what a typical NBA team will look like in
twenty years, if not sooner. "I think we are what the future will be.
There's no turning back any more than there is in signing Russian

hockey players or Latin American baseball players. Some believe in this some. Some people believe in it more. I happen to believe in it a lot and have since I started going over."

In the late eighties, Popovich was a Spurs' assistant to Larry Brown when he talked his general manager, Bob Bass, into sending him to Cologne, West Germany, for a European tournament. He was comfortable traveling abroad: His parents spoke Serbo-Croatian, he graduated from the Air Force Academy with a degree in Russian studies, and he'd played all over the world on armed forces teams. In Cologne, he felt like a pioneer—the only other NBA scout was Don Nelson, then the coach at Golden State, on the trail of Marciulionis. Popovich got his first live look at the stars of the Soviet and Yugoslav teams. "I fell in love with watching those guys practice, three hours in the afternoon, three hours more in the evening," he said. "It was all about learning, working on skills, repetition. It was a reflection of a system in which kids wanted to be coached, and that is so critical, the core of the matter and where we've gone wrong. Even though many of our kids are from modest means, they wouldn't believe where some of the European kids come from. It's meager. Our kids have become so entitled. Everybody says yes to them. Now the fundamental skills overseas have surpassed us in the U.S.—to what level people can disagree."

Larry Brown agreed, but he didn't blame the players. "Listen, I see guys in our league now who can't pass and catch," Brown said. "They don't even know what a pivot is, how to get into a defensive stance, and you know what? It's really not their fault. People say they don't want to be coached. I think they do, but when you have a culture that worships ESPN and highlights, this is what these kids know." It was one thing for coaches to speak out, but NBA legends, white and black, also complained about the way the game had been hijacked by the forces of self-interest. In his *New York Times* op-ed piece, Oscar Robertson wrote: "The question I am asked most frequently by youngsters who submit them to my Website is, 'What can I do to increase my vertical leap?' This captures in a nutshell the state of basketball today. Basketball is not a vertical game."

Nor was it in the Big O's day. With each succeeding decade, the athletes were bigger, stronger, faster. Even critics like myself who believed the excessively marketed dunk shot too often made a caricature of the sport had to acknowledge its thrilling athletic appeal, its pure entertainment value. However, when the argument was made that the game was now played above the rim and the outcry over the demise of old-school fundamentals was overdone and being used as a weapon against the African-American player, forgotten was that most of what occurred on the court was away from the rim, at ground level. In that regard, the geometry of the game and the need to understand it remained unchanged.

In the playgrounds of America, unfortunately, the notion of playing a structured, more team-oriented game somehow became a style for the athletically challenged, or to expand the stereotype, a system mostly designed for unathletic whites. In the NBA, teams employing schemes that stressed fluidity, ball and body movement, were said to be running the Princeton offense, even though, as Washington Wizards' coach Eddie Jordan said, "The reality of the quote-unquote Princeton offense is that it's not from Princeton as much as it's from the old Boston Celtics, the old Knicks championship teams. . . ."

In other words, from every NBA team that had succeeded across the decades, from one era to another. When I was covering the Knicks for the *New York Post,* there always seemed to be an ongoing debate about whether they should be a running team or a half-court team. One day, Red Holzman pulled me aside and offered some fatherly advice to an unseasoned reporter. "Don't write that shit," he said. "You want to be any good at this game, you'd just better know how to play, and that means doing it all." Holzman's message could be applied to the contemporary debate on fundamentals: The general formula for success was much the same for the vertically gifted as it was for future investment bankers.

A former Princeton center named Steve Goodrich realized this when he signed with New Jersey to be a spare part during the 2001–02 season. When Goodrich studied the Nets' playbook, he realized he'd already read it, in college. This was no coincidence, as the Nets' head coach, Byron Scott, and his lead assistant, Eddie Jordan, had worked with the former Princeton guru, Pete Carril, on the staff of the Sacramento Kings. "We used to talk all the time about the way the game was going, how sad it was," Jordan said. "We had fours [power forwards] and fives [centers] standing around, doing nothing. People always used to say that basketball was synonymous with ballet. Coach Carril and I were always saying, 'This is not how basketball should be played.'"

When Jordan began a brief tenure as the Kings' head coach, they decided to install the offense Carril had used at Princeton, which features dribble handoffs and backdoor cuts, and in which forwards and guards are virtually interchangeable in handling the ball. Blessed with excellent passing big men in Vlade Divac and Chris Webber, the Kings became a Western Conference power. Jordan moved east to join Scott's staff in New Jersey, and the team acquired one of the game's greatest intuitive players in Jason Kidd.

From where Goodrich sat, the Nets looked like an aerial version of his erstwhile and earthbound college team, exhibit A in the argument that the trends of the late twentieth century served only to typecast black players dominating major-college landscape and the NBA as too undisciplined to strive for precision and patience. The truth was that the Nets' offense enhanced talent more than inhibited it. "The offense is all about counters," Goodrich said. "Defender plays you close, you go backdoor. Guys at Princeton get a backdoor pass, we're pump-faking to get the ball up to rim. You take Kenyon Martin—he gets a bounce pass on the baseline, he's got unbelievable hands, so when he catches the ball, he's taking one stride and dunking. These guys are pros, the best in the world. A kid like Richard Jefferson, you tell him to cut, I mean, he cuts like a motherfucker."

For nearly their entire NBA history, the Nets were an NBA laughingstock, an embarrassment to Stern a few miles west of his fifteenth floor Manhattan perch in the Olympic Tower on Fifth Avenue. Overnight, spearheaded by Kidd, they were transformed into one of the league's most successful and esthetically pleasing teams. They won their first Eastern Conference title. Shaq and the Lakers swept them in the NBA Finals, but the Nets achieved a standing that few NBA teams managed in the early twenty-first century: They were celebrated in the New York metropolitan area for playing the game right. If only the league could have sent them to the next World Championships in Indianapolis that summer.

When the first team of American professionals finally lost, in the 2002 World Championships, they were beaten for the most part at a game they had long abandoned. Building a 20-point lead in the first half, sending us scrambling for the phones to alert our desks, Argentina's national team conducted a virtual layup drill, giving poor Ben Wallace, the U.S. frontcourt enforcer and NBA Defensive Player of the Year, a bad case of whiplash as cutters slipped behind him, left and right. "We kept switching when we weren't supposed to switch," point guard Andre Miller complained. "We were lost on defense." It was the night of September 4, 2002, at Conseco Fieldhouse when the NBA stars went down to their first defeat after fifty-eight straight wins, 87–80. In eight short years, supremacy had given way to superiority, then to survival, and, finally, to submission.

It didn't matter that Argentina, like Lithuania, had not a single player who had established himself in the NBA. "I remember George sitting in a room with the team, showing film of the Argentine team and I didn't think one of them was paying attention," said Gregg Popovich, an assistant coach to George Karl for those World Games. "They didn't believe a damn thing George was telling them, how good Argentina was, not until halftime.

You know, people are slow to see what's happening. Sometimes they don't want to see."

While historically significant, the event fell far short of the U.S. hockey win over the Soviets, or even the Lithuania semifinal game in Sydney. More than a miracle, this was inevitable, from the day of the ceremonial hanging of the first NBA jerseys in foreign markets, from the first satellite television feed. Even after the Argentina game, after the U.S. team went on to lose to the Serbs and to Spain, after the streets and stands around Conseco became a crush of Serbs bussed in by church groups all over the Midwest for the final against Argentina, the American rationale was that nothing had yet been proved. Young All-Stars such as Paul Pierce, Baron Davis, Shawn Marion, and Jermaine O'Neal were not America's absolute best. And what could we expect, some of the U.S. players asked, against experienced teams that had the advantage of familiarity?

"To a point, that's true," Popovich said. "Those other teams have played together many times in international competitions. But these aren't the old days, when the Soviets practiced year 'round." The foreign players were scattered far and wide during the season, just like the Americans. If Americans wanted to take comfort in the ready-made excuses, they were lying to themselves. It wasn't just different rules and styles accounting for these startling results. The athletic talent gap was also closing, an inescapable truth that should have hit home when Manu Ginobili took off on a fast break in the U.S.-Argentina game, only to confront the shot-block-minded Jermaine O'Neal angling in, bearing down.

Ginobili soared in for a layup from his natural southpaw side, made O'Neal commit, remained airborne as the big man flew by, switched hands, and scored on a neat reverse off glass. Argentine reporters, who would celebrate and weep openly after the game, erupted in cheers. From that moment on, the prototypical foreign player was no longer a mobility-challenged white boy in a crew cut. The story was no longer *Hoosiers* with subtitles.

"We have these mythical thoughts in our minds, like blacks can't play tennis or golf, white boys can't jump and Americans are better than Europeans," John Thompson told the *New York Daily News*. "That thought process is antiquated." These myths begot a cyclical myopia, also in evidence when the Williams sisters became the reigning divas of women's tennis. Critics pro and con agreed they were too strong, too athletic, for the undernourished country clubbers they were routinely trouncing. That is, until a cluster of focused Russian big babes with their own rags-to-riches stories came along to make a mockery of the racial typecasting.

Echoing Thompson was Larry Brown, who said, "I don't buy that any more, that the black athlete is automatically better. Nowitzki is every bit as athletic, Andrei Kirilenko, Pau Gasol, Ginobili. They can do all the things our guys do, even if it's not as flamboyant." Harry Edwards said the turn of events in international competitions had convinced him that however ingrained "black basketball" was in American culture, there was no more hiding from the world. "The way blacks changed the game, it's happening again," Edwards said. He worried less about the continuance of African-American dominance than about survival. "This isn't a wake-up call. It's the checkout," he said. "Look at what's happened in baseball."

It was hard to imagine African-Americans falling off in basketball the way they had in baseball, down to 9 percent for the 2005 season, roughly half the number from a decade past. Baseball, for a variety of reasons, was no longer in vogue in the inner city. That was far from the case with basketball, but the speculation and fears expressed by Edwards raised a fair question: Would it be such a tragedy if basketball's grip on young African-American males was somewhat loosened? "If we can get to the point where the NBA is not considered the black man's way out, that's better for the black community," said Nat Irvin, the futurist and executive professor from Wake Forest, and an African-American. "Every time I hear a kid say he wants to be something other than an NBA player, that's better. When I hear a kid say he wants to own an NBA team rather than play for one, that's really better."

I met Irvin at the same rookie orientation program at which Kenny Smith had raised the international rookies' ire; each of us had been invited by Billy Hunter of the Players Association to speak at a media seminar. Chatting as we waited for the event to begin, Irvin said he was fascinated by basketball's globalization: He saw it more as an important message to the African-American community than a threat, as a chance to learn and grow. "We're competing in a world in which there is a continuous search for global talent in all areas of business and technology," Irvin said. "We're competing in the classroom against Pakistanis, Indians, the Chinese." He wondered why people would question the motives of those who said Americans had fallen behind in basketball fundamentals. Weren't American students lagging behind in science and math? Weren't the international results—the basketball test scores—a fair indicator of the trends?

"When you can't pronounce the name of the player who doesn't look like you, there is a tendency to feel like you are losing something," Irvin said. "But there is something going on in the world that is larger than how we play ball." He noted that attitudes in sports tended to be regressive, harkening back to preferences many in the black community had for segregated schools and complaints from coaches of primarily black colleges when their recruiting base became the target of the larger football and basketball-playing universities.

He argued that the problem wasn't the potential loss of NBA jobs. It was the conditioning of too many black male minds that schoolwork was just an obstacle to overcome in order to continue playing ball. In our seminar, Irvin told the rookies that basketball's internationalization was no temporary trend, as Kenny Smith had suggested, and no "conspiratorial notion," based on the belief that "there are too many blacks and how can we get more white players into the game." He said what was happening in professional basketball was no different than what was occurring in most aspects of society. People were connected and dreams that were once uniquely American must now be shared. There was no doubt about it and no turning back. As Irvin spoke, my eyes wandered to the right side of the room, where Denver's Nikoloz Tskitishvili, the Georgian kid, was nodding, head down, and actually taking notes.

9

2002: Long Road to Riches

MY LIFE FLASHED BEFORE ME as Reed Salwen revved up his BMW, pushing and exceeding 100 miles per hour on the Italian autostrada while occasionally ignoring the road, glancing at the dash to determine the origin of the latest incoming call. "My second home," Salwen said, apparently referring to the left lane, which he vacated only upon the rearview sighting of another sleek European vehicle accelerating even faster than his.

Salwen, a thirty-six-year-old graduate of a Manhattan private school with degrees from McGill and Oxford, had rejected a more conventional career in what he called America's "fat, SUV culture" to be a professional sports agent, a multilingual hustler in a wireless headset. He was the European operative for a major New York area–based basketball broker, Marc Fleisher, most of whose clients were foreign. In the 2002 NBA draft, Fleisher and Salwen achieved a startling coup when the young Georgian, Nikoloz Tskitishvili, was selected fifth in the first round by Denver.

On our journey east, from Salwen's base in Milan to Treviso, just north of Venice, the calls from clients were constant: a Ukranian playing ball in France in need of a pep talk, a Frenchman in Bologna deserving a lecture, a Croat in Trieste begging for a bed from which his legs didn't dangle, a frantic German whose mother was accusing her estranged husband of rape. From Italian to Russian, Spanish to French, mixing in the occasional, "My man," Salwen chatted with a fraternal recognition, a cool confidence. Factoring in the easy smile and stylish shades, the most flattering imagery was Tom Cruise. Or, truer to character: Jerry Maguire gone continental.

"He didn't believe it," Salwen said when I asked how Tskitishvili, barely nineteen, reacted to the news that he'd gone from unheralded and largely unknown to the threshold of becoming a multimillionaire. "He kept saying, 'I can't believe this, I don't believe this.' Even when we were at the draft in New York and we told him it was happening, he was in shock when David Stern called him up and the fans were yelling and he was on television. I think it hit him then how much of a big deal it was. That's what's interesting about what we do because all these kids—Serbia, Croatia, Georgia—they want to be basketball players and now they want to be NBA players but for them it can't be like it is in the U.S., it just can't be, because they have no idea what a big deal it is, what a show, until they get here and they see the American players with their posses and pearls. It's another world for them and given where they come from, it is almost unfathomable."

I found myself fascinated by the merging of these cultures, the trails foreign players were blazing and, after my discussions with Nat Irvin, the impact—psychological and otherwise—they were having on the African-American community. Several weeks after meeting Tskitishvili at predraft player interviews, I immediately thought of him when an editor at the *Times* asked if I had interest in contributing to a front-page series the newspaper was developing on the global purview of American influence.

My assignment would be a sports/entertainment piece, a story reported over several months, that would explore the evolving basketball phenomenon and how it was shaping attitudes about America abroad. The real attraction for me after a decade of near-obsessive fascination with international basketball was the opportunity to go to Europe to learn why and how globalization was working. I could not really write about the changes in the sport with any serious degree of expertise until I saw for myself where these kids were coming from, reported the story from their side of the pond.

I called Marc Fleisher, a longtime industry acquaintance whose family was deeply rooted in NBA history. His father, Larry, steered the players' union during the sports labor movement of the sixties and seventies that, especially in the NBA's case, helped empower the black athlete. The Fleisher name also figured prominently in the league's more contemporary changes: In the late eighties, about the time David Stern began to market his league abroad, Larry Fleisher envisioned Europe as an eventual talent pipeline. Following his death in May 1989, sons Marc and Eric completed negotiations their father had begun with Vlade Divac, and Divac, along with Sarunas Marciulionis, opened the door for foreign players to become impact NBA players without attending an American university. Finally, in 1995, during a strategic split that led to the brothers' bitter and litigious breakup, Eric Fleisher joined up with a high-school senior out of Chicago named Kevin Garnett and steered him into the NBA. Clearly, Tskitishvili had Garnett, who happened to be his favorite player growing up in Tbilisi, to thank for beginning the process of NBA teams drafting more on potential than performance.

In my conversation with Fleisher, he mentioned another intriguing wrinkle to the Tskitishvili story: He recently had signed another Georgian from Tbilisi, sixteen-year-old Manuchar Markoishvili, and placed him with Benetton Treviso, one of the richer European professional clubs and exactly the place where Tskitishvili had been tagged and identified the previous year. Fleisher agreed to introduce me to Reed Salwen, who in turn connected me to a Georgian scout who had tipped Salwen off on Tskitishvili when Tskitishvili was a scrawny seventeen-year-old, soaring toward seven feet tall, with raw but unmistakable skills and a lightness of foot that could be traced to preadolescent membership in a Tbilisi dance troupe. Tbilisi to Treviso to Denver: The markers were in place to follow the yellow-brick road, albeit in reverse.

My editor at the *Times* loved the layered texture of the story, of Tskitishvili's coming-of-age as war was literally being waged in the streets of Tbilisi, as the impoverished republic lurched toward quasidemocracy. When Tskitishvili was two years old, his father died in an auto wreck. With a three-year, $7 million contract, Tskitishvili was suddenly the affluent family breadwinner, just like so many young African-American basketball stars I'd been covering for more than two decades. But, in Georgia, that distinction could be complicated and frightening, given the wave of kidnappings of people of money and influence. From Reed Salwen, I learned that the college-age brother of Georgia's national soccer team star, Kakha Kaladze, had been abducted and held for $600,000 by bandits operating near the border with Chechnya, also the redoubt of anti-Kremlin jihadists. In Denver, the Nuggets were already working with federal authorities to obtain visas for Tskitishvili's mother and twelve-year-old half-brother.

NBA training camps were just opening for the 2002–03 season as I completed travel plans with a *Times* photographer, Rick Perry, for the kind of assignment I found exhilarating, an opportunity to stretch out and roam far from the predictability and provincialism of the mainstream sports calendar. On the trip to Italy and Georgia, I would be counting more on my wits, curiosity, and, while on the autostrada, Salwen's Grand Prix driving skills. Our first stop: La Ghirada, the sprawling Benetton sports complex on the outskirts of Treviso, where the clothing giant housed and trained its company-sponsored professional teams in soccer, volleyball, and basketball. As if to mimic, or mock, the American developmental system, the Benetton people called it their campus.

•   •   •

At sixteen, Manuchar Markoishvili had the face of a cherub that was attached to the thick and muscular body of a thirty-year-old man. He was six-six, a shooting guard, and though Benetton, like most European clubs, had a junior team for players his age, the newly arrived Georgian boy was already on the varsity roster, slated to play and travel across the continent with men who, in some cases, were double his age.

Back in Tbilisi, he said he had been a good student, but had ended his conventional schooling at fifteen to play for a Georgian pro team in the Black Sea town of Batumi, where he earned the equivalent of a few hundred dollars a month. "I wanted to be a basketball player," he said. Abroad, I quickly realized that the talent hunt was unburdened by the ethical debate regarding the need for a purely amateur experience, much less a college degree or high-school diploma. Markoishvili's father had a history degree but had opted for a career as a basketball coach. His mother taught school. He described the family as middle class, which, in Georgia, did not translate into four bedrooms with two SUVs parked in the driveway. "People who go to college don't make a lot of money in Georgia," Markoishvili said. Not like basketball players, at least those who made it big in the States. "I remember reading that Shaquille O'Neal signed for seventy-six million dollars a few years ago," he recalled. "They said in the paper that O'Neal has more money than the whole Georgian economy."

Even as a teenage trainee in Treviso, Markoishvili's $25,000 salary, most of which he sent home, represented a small fortune by Georgian standards. He was also studying Italian in classes provided by the Benetton organization in a variety of subjects for its junior players, absorbing English, and living in a dormlike cubicle, where the only visible reading material was an Italian–Georgian dictionary, an Italian NBA magazine, and the Bible he brought from home. He ate free at the campus restaurant.

"He doesn't have to worry about anything except basketball and he is lucky to be here," said Ettore Messina, the Benetton coach, a middle-aged man with dark, movie-star looks, who's been a longtime fixture around the Italian game. The next night, Benetton began its Euro League season at the Palaverde, an austere arena with five thousand seats constructed for elves, all painted Benetton green. Messina sent Markoishvili into the game for the final 2 minutes and 35 seconds of a 21-point rout of the French club, Pau Orthez. He made one steal, had his first shot blocked, and later, over dinner with the team at a restaurant owned by one of its veteran players, downed Cokes while the veterans sipped wine and argued over who would pick up his tab and return the teenager to his room.

One of his teammates, an American, considered young Markoishvili an excellent example of why the U.S. basketball establishment needed to wake up and get its act together. "I talk to guys from the States and they say, 'Oh, we only lost at the World Championships last summer because we didn't have Shaq, we didn't have Kobe,'" said Trajan Langdon, the former Duke star and one of Benetton's two allowed American imports that season. "That's missing the point. Shaq's not going to play forever. I tell guys back home they'd better realize what's happening over here. You look at Manuchar, he's only a kid but he's practicing every day against experienced guys in an environment where the competition is tougher than college."

Benetton played two games a week, one in the Euro League, the other in the Italian League. That left plenty of time for practice, up to three hours in the afternoon and three more at night on most off days. And that was exactly the point: practice. For the typical young professional, the European system was far more instructional—with no emphasis on winning for junior-team players—compared to the AAU-sponsored tournaments and the recruiting and job-seeking rat race to produce immediate NCAA results back in the States. "Here, it's all about the practice and everybody does the same things," said Messina. "We don't tell the big guy, 'Go under the basket and get the rebound.' They learn to dribble, pass, shoot three-pointers. Nobody comes in and says, 'I'm the star. Just give me the ball.'"

With all the talk about fundamentals following the American flop in Indianapolis, I asked Messina if the abrupt turn of events in international play had surprised him. He shook his head. "Every year, it gets closer and now the Americans can't think, 'We have better athletes,' and put together a team in ten days like they did in ninety-two, when they were golfing and having a good time. Nobody is anymore intimidated." In his previous job in Bologna, Messina had coached Manu Ginobili, the Argentine who, in fall 2002, was beginning his first San Antonio training camp. After watching Spain's Pau Gasol make the successful leap to the NBA the previous season, Messina foresaw stardom in the NBA for Ginobili. "I will tell you two very strange things and hopefully you will not think I am crazy," Messina said. "I think Ginobili can have a great impact in terms of emotion, like Magic Johnson had on Jabbar. Tim Duncan, he's a quiet player, that's what I see on TV. With the intensity of Ginobili's game, the way he plays every day, and with the eighty-two-game routine, he will be a surprise, because when the other players are going through the motions, he will be playing all out, every night. He is hungry to prove that a kid from Argentina belongs."

As it turned out, Messina was right. With his unorthodox mix of unbridled physicality and athleticism, Ginobili was immediately an impact player, eventually an All-Star, the swashbuckling embodiment of the whole foreign movement and the dislodging of the United States as the unchallenged superpower in international play. "Allow me to make the comparison—even though maybe it's not politically correct—but it's like Vietnam," Messina said. "You go there, you think you have everything you need and all of a sudden—boom, boom—they come out of places you don't even know or see and all of a sudden, you start questioning your own organization, your leadership. Unless you start sending all the superstars and they put in the work, it's only going to get worse."

What Messina was saying was that the United States was suffering the effects of arrogance and indulgence, not a surprising point of view at a time when many Europeans saw Americans as wanting everything both ways. American-bred players sought to reap the benefits of global marketing without making the competitive sacrifices just as, in a more serious realm, Americans demanded to win the war on terrorism hatched in countries rich on U.S. oil receipts while continuing to flood their highways with gas-guzzling vehicles. If the behavior of American basketball stars was a reflection of the times, it could also be argued that Kobe Bryant was just following the lead of the unilateralist in the White House when he alienated Shaq and others who had been his allies for the chance to shake and bake, shock and awe, on his own terms.

While veteran coaches like Larry Brown pined for the days when college underclassmen worked on their skills and waited their turn, the view from Europe was that the American system had become inimical to comprehensive development. It had broken down because its values were upside down, lavishing undue enticements and empowerment on impressionable teenagers at the precise time they need an apprenticeship to better grasp the precepts of team play. In the United States, fame precedes knowledge. Style obscures substance. Power overrides practice. Years ago, Messina said, any major college player could excel in a European professional league. "Now if you get a player from college, he doesn't know the fundamentals, he's not ready to play," he said. "Once the big pride of Americans was the education and teaching but it's no more like that. It's 'What are you going to give me?' "

I asked Messina if he had heard the Dajuan Wagner story, about the high-school superstar in Camden, New Jersey, who, in January 2001, was allowed by his coach to score 100 points in a 90-point blowout. The coach said he felt he owed it to Wagner for all he'd done for the school. When Wagner, undersized for a shooting guard at six-three, should have been setting up the scrubs and honing his playmaking skills, he was given a green light to embellish his legend at the expense of basic sportsmanship and his own personal growth. Then John Calipari begged Wagner to attend Memphis University. Calipari also hired Wagner's father and handed a scholarship to his best friend, all for the privilege of coaching Wagner for one season before he entered the NBA draft. The Wagner saga was a microcosm of everything wrong with the American approach. "I have many friends who coach in the U.S., who coach the international competitions," Messina said. "They say the players are too spoiled. They want the attention. They want to shoot, be on TV and they've got leverage: 'You don't want me? No problem, I'll go someplace else, I'll go to another team, another school, I'll get drafted.'"

An experience I had writing a series of columns about a Brooklyn prodigy named Lenny Cooke came to mind. Cooke, who was touted à la LeBron a year or two sooner, attended several high schools, including one in the wealthy suburban enclave of Old Tappan, New Jersey, where he lived with a former teammate's mother, who had managed their AAU team. Debbie Bortner wanted to help Cooke straighten out his academic life so that he might qualify for a Division I program, but soon he grew hostile to her, resisting her attempts to keep him in school and off the Brooklyn streets. "She just wants my money when I make the league," Cooke told me one day, sitting right in Bortner's kitchen, failing to notice that Bortner's home was palatial and, married to a wealthy man, she already lived like a queen. Not surprisingly, Cooke was soon gone, in the clutches of the next benefactor.

With so many industry climbers at their heels, how could these kids ever really know whom to trust? Was it really the American teenagers' fault when standard measures of discipline and the logical developmental progression were so out of whack? Messina said he couldn't answer the deeper philosophical questions. He only knew, "The world is developing players, and, from what I see in America, the level is not even close to what it used to be. They all dunk, all jump, all do the physical things, but they don't shoot or handle the ball that well. They are sending a lot of players to these competitions now who technically are so-so."

That didn't mean every man-child named Manuchar was

going to cash in a lottery ticket, make it all the way to the NBA, where the level of athleticism was still well beyond the reach of most. "If he were a seven-footer, with talent, everybody in the NBA has an opening," Messina said. "At his position, he will be powerful but everything will depend on his quickness when he will be twenty, twenty-one. He reminds me of Ginobili, with how hard he works, but Ginobili had lateral quickness, the explosiveness that Manuchar doesn't have. At this point, I would say he has a chance."

That was all Markoishvili was asking for, the same opportunity as any American kid, from Crown Heights to Compton. Tskitishvili, who had played ball with Markoishvili's older brother, was already calling from Denver to tell him about the trappings of NBA life—the Lincoln Navigator sport utility vehicle with the customized television, the $2,800 a month luxury condo in a trendy suburb called Cherry Creek, the amazing "basketball halls" with roomy seats for twenty thousand fans. Tskitishvili also reminded him that no one knew or could even pronounce his name when he'd arrived in Treviso in the fall of 2001. Months later, after playing sparingly, scoring 73 points in 11 games, averaging a modest 12.7 minutes, he was shaking hands with David Stern, proof beyond a doubt that places like Treviso were as much an itinerant stop along the NBA scouting trail as old Tobacco Road.

With Tskitishvili delivered to Denver, with the number of foreign players increasing every year, with the results of the World Championships leaping off the pages of the newspapers, why wouldn't Markoishvili indulge in the dream? On our last night in Treviso, as we chatted over dinner, his English a lot better than my Georgian or Russian, I asked Markoishvili if he had a favorite American film. He thought for a while and then remembered one he had rented in Tbilisi, about gangsters who were Jewish and had terrorized the streets of old New York. "Robert De Niro?" I asked him. "Yes, yes, De Niro," he said, although I couldn't remember the name of the film until the following night, during a bumpy connecting flight from Vienna to Tbilisi: *"Once Upon a Time in America."*

The moment we approached the cluster of buildings in which Nikoloz Tskitishvili had grown up, I understood what the well-traveled Reed Salwen had meant when he tried to prepare us for Tbilisi, when he'd said that the foreign players had every reason to be as hungry, as focused, as ours. "I've seen Compton," he said. "It's still not Russia. It's not Georgia." The buildings were rotting hulks, Soviet-style architectural blemishes across an otherwise undulating, scenic landscape that made the Staten Island housing project I'd grown up in look like Trump Tower. There was no glass in the windows of the dank common areas, crumbling cement staircases, a tiny elevator illuminated by one blinking bare bulb. A courtyard served as an improvised parking area for a few rusted sedans and a basketball court with a backboard that was attached to a pole and constructed of thin sheets of wood separated by cracks of light.

Here, Tskitishvili launched his first shots and, now, his twelve-year-old half-brother, Giorgi, played three-on-three with neighborhood friends, wearing a Denver Nuggets' jersey with his brother's nickname—Tskita—on the back. Upstairs, on the sixth floor of 2 Nutsubidze Plato, Guliko Tskitishvili craned her neck outside on the narrow terrace to check on her son. The steady pounding of the basketball could be heard on the cracked cement of the ramshackle play area, but she had to see for herself. She had to be sure he was there. "I don't worry for me, only if they will take Giorgi," she said, referring to the threat of abduction, however imagined or real, that she never spoke of in front of the boy to spare him the fear. "When he plays in the yard, I am always near."

Her home captured the complexities of Georgian life, then and now, from a relatively stable standard of living on the Communist dole to independence and the pursuit of democracy with a collapsed economy and no safety net. When the state-funded complex was built in the early eighties, the location, on a hill overlooking old Tbilisi, was a sign of prestige. "We are people of art," Guliko said, explaining with the help of a translator that she, like her Nikoloz, had danced professionally as a younger woman, and sang, while her late husband, Misha, was a singer and actor before his fatal auto accident in 1985. Her daughter, Nino, was a model who, in 1997, competed in a European beauty pageant as Miss Georgia. "We own the apartment," she said. "We take care of it, but outside, after the Communists fell, nobody has the money or the desire to do anything."

A tall, robust woman, Guliko Tskitishvili was laying out a Georgian-style spread, or *supra,* with national delicacies like *khachapuri,* a breaded cheese pie, and *khinkali,* a meat dumpling, under a striking chandelier. Behind the table stood an upright piano. Tastefully done portraits of the children adorned the walls. The rare decorative concession to her son's vocation was a basketball, autographed by David Stern, that sat in a bowl attached to a gold-plated ornamental base. The small rooms were meticulously neat, though there was only one bedroom, which for a time was shared by Guliko and her three children, until Nino married and a sprouting Nikoloz fled to a small alcove where Guliko's sister now slept. A television faced a convertible sofa and there was a small satellite dish on the terrace. I could imagine Nikoloz as a boy of Giorgi's age, curled up in the wee hours, glued to the set as Michael Jordan and the Bulls nailed down the NBA championship from another world, thousands of miles away.

Our visit seemed to have been cause for much preparation and celebration, for dinners organized by Zurab Bokolishvili, a local sports entrepreneur and agent who had met Reed Salwen when the American, then employed by Nike and based in Moscow, visited Tbilisi following the Soviet collapse to explore the potential for a new sneaker franchise. Bokolishvili, who represented several Georgian athletes and maintained an office in Moscow, had a shaved head, a penchant for finely tailored suits, and breezed about town in a Dodge Durango with his ubiquitous and brawny friend George, later identified as an investigator for the Georgian Ministry of Internal Affairs, at the wheel.

The dinners were veritable feasts, with much consumption of Georgian wine and many emotional and verbose toasts, commenced by the table's *tamada,* or toastmaster, traditionally a male and, in this case, Bokolishvili. Had they'd heard that American sportswriters expected to be fed? "We make interviews later," he repeated whenever Rick and I expressed interest in exploring the city and the local basketball community. Having been forewarned by Salwen that Georgians were a poor but proud people, that it was customary to feed and fuss over guests, we acceded to Bokolishvili's wishes and even accepted his offer to attend a European Cup qualifying soccer grudge match between Georgia and Russia.

The downtown stadium, holding about forty thousand, was free of frills, to say the least. The food concessions were wrinkled old women, huddled on the ground, selling bread. The experience symbolized the state of Georgian sociopolitical affairs—murky most of the time and occasionally dark. At halftime of the soccer match, with the score 0–0, the stadium lights died. "Maybe politics," Bokolishvili said, considering the Russians were controlling play. A defeat for Georgia would have meant likely elimination and lights were shining elsewhere in a city infamous for power outages, among other daily hardships. Almost an hour later, the stadium having somehow survived the rampant lighting of newspapers into flaming torches in a crowd of chain smokers, it emptied, despite no announcement of the game's postponement. The fans filed quietly into the street, at least until the motorcade of the soon-to-be deposed President Eduard Shevardnadze exited a stadium ramp and became the target for the frustrations of this night, and others.

With a way-of-life shrug, Bokolishvili made his way to the Dodge Durango, parked across the street, right on the sidewalk, with the apparent blessing of the attendant police. "Everybody knows everybody," he said, as George tore through town at hair-raising speeds, defying oncoming traffic in order to pass, and treating red lights as mere suggestions. When Rick and I meekly inquired about rules of the road, Bokolishvili laughed. "No problem for us," he said, which we took as a boast that men with connections in the right places and handguns in their waistbands need not worry about potential consequences, or a simple assurance that this was just what passed here for expert driving.

When we decided to explore on our own, the subway seemed much safer despite our navigational and linguistic handicaps. As we rode long escalators that led deep below street level, I had flashbacks to my own early childhood in New York City, riding the trains in Brooklyn and Manhattan with my parents. Here, the subways looked and smelled just like the 1950s, and the token—the one souvenir I brought home—seemed to best symbolize the plainness of this place that time had apparently forgot: a red plastic chip, right out of a child's bingo game. I couldn't help but think that even an NBA minimum salary in a city like Tbilisi would be enough to live like a king.

There was little state money to renovate anything, least of all the 2,500-seat Vere Basketball Hall, which Bokolishvili finally delivered us to, as promised, on a warm October afternoon, a Georgian holiday, when eleven- and twelve-year-old boys were engaged in a full-court scrimmage in the dusty gym that was legendary for its lack of serviceable heat. "No coaches in America would train in such cold," said Vaja Kvarachelia, already dreading winter. "But there is no money, so the boys wear their sweatpants. We do the best we can."

And when it was enough to send a young man off to a pro league in Europe and now the United States, the pride alone was enough to radiate the gym for weeks. A sad-eyed man with a long, narrow face, Kvarachelia, forty-one, was Tskitishvili's first coach, and volunteer surrogate father. A native of the breakaway northwest province of Abkhazia, a veteran of the 1990s war there that displaced a quarter-million Georgians, Kvarachelia said that, because he was orphaned by his fifth birthday, he was especially sympathetic to Tskitishvili when he began working with the athletic boy at thirteen. "I was always jealous of those children who had fathers, so when I saw how gifted a child he was I always wanted to somehow substitute for his loss," he said. In the dark and cold, Kvarachelia would walk his prize pupil home, an hour's journey, so his mother wouldn't worry. He would fill the disbelieving teenager's head with possibilities of going beyond the Georgian league and Europe and all the way across the Atlantic. "Because of the dance I could see his movement, I felt it was destiny," Kvarachelia said.

The raspy-voiced coach's eyes welled with tears, and it struck me that Tskitishvili's story was no different from so many others I had heard and reported on through the years of covering basketball in the States, from Micheal Ray Richardson to LeBron James: humble roots, father gone, taken under wing by coach—the urban fairy tale with even greater odds. In this case, Kvarachelia was admittedly worried that it was all happening too fast. He used to tell Tskitishvili: "Playing in America is like playing in the jungle." However lacking in American racial etiquette, Kvarachelia intuitively knew the NBA transition would be difficult for a young man to whom aggression and entitlement had never come easy, who had little practical game experience, and who was carrying the vested hopes of people who drafted him and represented him, and of the youngsters coming up behind him.

To the Georgians we had met, Tskitishvili was more than a ballplayer. Thanks to his high draft standing, he was, or had the potential to be, Georgia's most prominent ambassador to the world's greatest superpower, whose friendship, assistance, and investment their country desperately sought. His old coach, who himself was looking forward to visiting Denver and stepping inside the glamorous basketball hall known as the Pepsi Center, only hoped that people would have patience, expect no instant miracles, but the high draft position had already gone to everyone's head, along with the wine. Back at 2 Nutsubidze Plato, where Guliko Tskitishvili's guests had settled in to eat, Zurab

Bokolishvili raised his glass and launched into another fervent tribute. "To Nika, our great natural resource," he said. "In one or two years, even better than Nowitzki."

Kenny Smith had this part right: There was only one Dirk Nowitzki, in the same way there was only one Michael Jordan. From the moment he made his debut in the 2002–03 season, checking into the Nuggets' opener in Minneapolis to match up against Kevin Garnett, it was apparent that Tskitishvili was not ready to be Nowitzki or even an NBA player. Far from open arms, Garnett welcomed him with profane invective: "Do you know who the fuck I am?" ('Course he did.) "You can't fucking guard me!" (No, he couldn't.) Tskitishvili was jolted from a state of charming and contented reverence that had moved him to literally reach out and touch Michael Jordan during a preseason game against the Washington Wizards because, as he explained, "I just had to."

After the game in Minneapolis, the Nuggets returned to Denver, landing in a Halloween snowstorm, and Tskitishvili drove to a downtown hotel to meet his mother and half-brother, who had arrived with newly minted visas that day from Tbilisi. The reunion turned out to be the highlight of his two and one-half years in Denver. By the following season, Carmelo Anthony was the new rookie sheriff in town, and one who came NCAA-championship ready to light up scoreboards all over the league. Tskitishvili, never the star or even a regular contributor on any team, hung on the perimeter of the Nuggets' offense when given spare minutes, symbolically positioned on the NBA threshold, as if waiting for an invitation to step inside. Then he drifted to the end of the bench, where he was conveniently ignored and soon forgotten. By the middle of the 2004–05 season, the third and final year of Tskitishvili's contract, he was dispirited, nearly broken, when we caught up before a game in New Jersey.

The Denver front office executives who treated him like royalty upon his arrival barely spoke to him anymore, he said. His half-brother, homesick and pained by Tskitishvili's virtual nonstatus, returned to live in Tbilisi, and was followed months later by his mother. Sportswriters in Denver and elsewhere routinely called him a waste of a number-five pick, a bust at twenty-one. In a very American fit of pique, he demanded to be traded and fired his agents, Fleisher and Salwen. "How can I get better when I never play?" he pleaded.

It was a good question, and it spoke directly to the issue of the NBA training vacuum. Tskitishvili was like any American high-school kid who wasn't a developmental freak of nature, a LeBron James or Amare Stoudemire, and who needed to play regularly in a more nurturing environment. He would have been better off seasoning in Europe another two years, like Ginobili or Andrei Kirilenko or New Jersey's twenty-one-year-old Serbian seven-footer, Nenad Krstic, who began the 2004–05 season as a rookie benchwarmer and finished it looking like a young Vlade Divac. But Tskitishvili's high draft standing, as with the Pistons' Darko Milicic, demanded he come over immediately to, in effect, justify himself.

Taken second in the 2003 draft at eighteen, Milicic was experiencing the same frustration in Detroit, where Larry Brown was more concerned with winning, and then defending, a championship than sacrificing minutes to mentor his seven-foot Serbian wunderkind, whose work ethic, the coach said, was as immature as his body. "It's really hurt him coming over when he did," Brown said. "We're playing three, four games in five nights, and this kid doesn't get to play and doesn't even get to practice." Brown wished he could send Milicic to the developmental league the NBA launched in 2001 but it was restricted to players twenty and older, creating an inane paradox whereby an eighteen-year-old could play with the big boys but not in the minors. "I want to see us be able to get together with a New Jersey or a New York and say, 'You pick a coach and we'll pick a coach and we'll develop a style where these kids can learn,'" Brown said.

It made so much sense but, like so many other good ideas in sports, the concept was trapped in limbo between management and labor. Billy Hunter, the union's executive director, disagreed with the baseball minor-league comparison and was unenthusiastic about granting teams so-called farm-outs rights of players not deemed ready for NBA duty. "Jermaine O'Neal will tell you that he got better playing in practice in Portland against Arvydas Sabonis," Hunter said. "NBA players are prodigies, superior athletes, and the competition in a minor league isn't good enough to get them ready." Canvassing the players on this issue, Hunter said he asked Darko Milicic if he would have preferred to be playing in the developmental league to sitting on the Pistons' bench. "In front of his teammates, he said he wouldn't have even come if it meant playing in a minor league," Hunter said. "He would've stayed in Europe."

More than a logically thought-out position, this was more the consequence of a system that conditioned players to view apprenticeship as an insult. Having seen both Milicic and Tskitishvili play, albeit sparingly, I was fairly certain that what they most needed, if only for a year, was time on the floor to work on their game skills and confidence. "There's no substitute for doing it in a game, any game," said Chris Mullin, the Golden State Warriors' chief basketball executive who, in early 2005, acquired Tskitishvili from Denver. The Warriors were a young, improving team but one that already had two young six-eleven Euros, Andris Biedrins of Latvia and Zarko Cabarkapa of Serbia-Montenegro, ahead of Tskitishvili on the depth chart. Mullin said he liked Tskitishvili's athleticism, his practice habits, but admitted that didn't mean much. "You've got to show the toughness, the ability to make a shot when you get bumped, or have a hand in your face, or very soon you go from 'he's not doing it' to 'he can't do it,'" Mullin said.

The trick for evaluating prospects is to avoid all stereotypes, be willing to look far and wide and accept the possibility that a mistake could be made on anyone from anywhere. "The international players' skill level is attractive and our system may have gone awry, too heavy on athleticism, but somewhere in the middle is where you find the player," Mullin said. He didn't believe that the unhappy early returns on Tskitishvili (who would sign a minimum NBA contract for the 2005–06 season with Minnesota, Kevin Garnett's team) or Milicic would turn NBA teams off to importing more foreign goods. "I don't see it closing down," Mullin said. "Too many guys have succeeded now and they are the role models for the foreign kids to come."

Indeed, the rage of the 2004–05 college season, on his way to being selected first in the 2005 draft by Milwaukee after his sophomore year at Utah, was the seven-footer, Andrew Bogut, whose Croat parents immigrated to Australia as teenagers in the 1970s. Bogut's hero, the fuel to his boyhood NBA fantasy, was the late Drazen Petrovic, reported *Sports Illustrated*. When I read the story, it reminded me of a visit I made to the national sports institute in Paris in 2003 while covering the French Open. Back in the States, the NBA Finals were beginning in San Antonio, whose point guard, Tony Parker, had come through the French system. That afternoon, the director of the institute let me tag along on a tour with fourteen-year-old prospective enrollees. They were all wearing Parker jerseys, which, I was told, were flying off racks in Parisian sports shops.

"You look around the league and you can name the foreign players who are the best players on their teams—Nowitzki, Gasol, Kirilenko—and then you have a whole bunch of impact guys like Stojakovic, Ginobili, Parker," said Marc Fleisher, whose client list included Kirilenko and Parker. He called the 2005 foreign class not especially laden with spellbinding talent, and yet, beyond Bogut, six other players born outside the United States were taken in the first round. Eighteen were selected in the two-round draft overall. On draft night, Dick Vitale complained bitterly on ESPN that American college players were being unfairly bypassed, arguing that Yao Ming was the only import of impact. Nobody on the esteemed panel of analysts bothered to remind Vitale of Nowitzki, Ginobili, Kirilenko, or Gasol. For many, the blinders of ignorance or self-interest are still fastened tight.

As for 2006 and beyond, I conducted my own unscientific Internet investigation and found scores of foreign names among those being projected for future NBA duty, from Argentina to Asia. I recognized only one, though, an eighteen-year-old Georgian shooting guard and star of the country's national junior team: Manuchar Markoishvili. Which convinced me that in a grand scheme of things, Nikoloz Tskitishvili had already succeeded, if not as an NBA player, then as a basketball citizen of the earth, more proof that it was possible for the legions of foreign boys tall and skilled. Nothing was guaranteed in America, in the NBA, but Tskitishvili had been given his crack at the league of opulence in the land of opportunity, as the fifth player drafted, as a wide-eyed kid who once had a dream and cashed his lottery ticket from a game now marketed and played just about anywhere in the whole, wide world.

10

2004–05: The Big Fix

RICHARD JEFFERSON caught my attention one day during the 2004–05 season, when he said the reaction to the U.S. bronze-medal finish at the Athens Olympics "bordered on racism." Jefferson, the New Jersey Nets' talented and sharp-witted small forward, was trying to explain what he meant but was wilting in the crucible of sports-talk radio. "I didn't really get a chance," he complained a few days later when I asked him at a Nets' practice why he seemed to back off when challenged on air. "It was, 'Oh, come on, how can you say that? You guys won the bronze medal. You embarrassed your country. What are you talking about?' "

Fast becoming one of the NBA's shining lights, until sidelined with a broken wrist late in 2004, Jefferson almost always had something on his mind that he wanted to talk about and was well worth listening to. The son of a one-time welfare mother turned college English professor, Jefferson played a flamboyant aerial game, enjoyed a good round of trash talk as much as anyone but, like Jermaine O'Neal, was ready in a heartbeat to confront those who would try to reduce him to a stereotype, who would characterize him as a belligerent and tattooed gansta in baggy gym shorts. Yes, he enjoyed listening to rap music but his collection also happened to include a wide range of styles, from James Brown to Fleetwood Mac.

So what, exactly, did Jefferson mean when he contended that the general reaction to the three-defeat flameout in Athens was borderline racism? "We kind of felt like we were, you know, in a cage, people picking us apart," Jefferson told me. "My thing is when we win, well, we're supposed to. Whenever we lose, we're lazy and unpatriotic. Is that racist? I don't know, but it seemed that a lot of people were just very anxious to tear down twelve young black men."

Concurring was union chief Billy Hunter, who said his blood boiled when he read headlines that calculated the combined salaries of the players and called them "the 80-something million-dollar bronze medalists." The U.S. team had hit the ground stumbling in Europe, getting blown out by Italy, a country that hadn't even qualified for the Olympics, in an exhibition tuneup. The Americans began the Games by getting whacked by a Puerto Rico team they had whipped a couple of weeks earlier during training camp. They dropped a second game in the preliminary round, when Lithuania gained a measure of revenge from the Sydney semifinal, and were easily handled in the semis by Manu Ginobili and Argentina, the gold-medal winner.

Once again, the basketball world watched with amazement as the Americans shrank when confronted by a sagging zone defense. It watched as the hastily created U.S. team failed to capitalize on the double and triple teams drawn by Tim Duncan, and as it couldn't dominate slick-passing and shooting opponents on defense, the way its pre-Sydney predecessors had done. Billy Hunter acknowledged the Athens results were not what he had hoped for, but, like Jefferson, he didn't appreciate the accusatory tenor of the response. Was there a lingering effect created by the finger-wagging and crotch-grabbing players of Toronto and Sydney vintage? Probably. Did Jefferson and his teammates bear the brunt of the resentment for those who had committed to the cause and played in the Tournament of the Americas in Puerto Rico the previous summer only to beg off of Athens? Undoubtedly. Some, including Jermaine O'Neal, made no bones about not wanting to deal with the threat of a terrorist attack, which didn't exactly make the NBA look like the home of the brave. Jefferson's argument was that those who finally did go—Next Generation linchpins LeBron James, Carmelo Anthony, Dwyane Wade, and Amare Stoudemire among them—should have been applauded, not hooted, regardless of the outcome. "They had to go through thirty-four people to find twelve that would play and then, when we lose, we become 'those guys?'" Jefferson said.

For family reasons, the Athens Olympics were the first I didn't cover, winter or summer, since 1988. All the games were shown on live television, however; the satellite images did not lie. The Americans—all NBA impact players of varying degrees, if not internationally experienced—were much less the sum of their celebrated parts. A lack of practice time didn't help, though there also was the usual NBA-grapevine dissatisfaction with the attitude and behavior of some players. Larry Brown, the losing Olympic coach weeks after winning his first NBA title with the Pistons, resumed his love-hate relationship with his old Philadelphia sparring mate, Allen Iverson, who in many ways was the classic embodiment of the American basketball system. Wildly talented and fearless, willing to hurl his 165 pounds into men at least 100 pounds heavier night after night along the NBA trail, Iverson also had driven Brown and other coaches crazy with his undisciplined practice habits and made the league's home office crowd nervous with an urban persona that gave him more "street cred" than any other NBA player.

"It shows that great players can be wrapped—pardon the expression—in very small packages," Stern quipped when he presented Iverson with the MVP trophy after the 2001 All-Star Game. Hunter said he'd been badgering the league for years to give in and allow Iverson to play for the national team. In Athens, Iverson was Brown's most ferocious competitor, the team's most verbal and honest broker, but Brown also believed that he was a less-than-exemplary influence on the impressionable Anthony and James. "They followed him, they didn't handle the situation well, they were too worried about their playing time," Brown said. "I don't blame any of those kids. They're all special players and they're having great years but all the dribble-drive skills they possess don't matter against a zone, when the foreign teams have big guys who just sit in there, make you shoot a jump shot. And because we had the kids, we had no real point guard, no shooters, no role players."

In so many words, Brown was suggesting that the inclusion of the self-labeled Young Gunners, much as they represented the sport's American-born future and graduated to indisputable stardom in 2004–05, was just yet another case, and arguably the most telling example, of NBA market-to-the-max mentality. This was an unfortunate policy that made a priority of global jersey sales when what U.S.A. Basketball desperately needed was less style and more experience and skill, a team that may not have created a buzz but would have been able to shoot the ball. Though the U.S. vulnerability in international play actually advanced Stern's blueprint for global penetration, enhanced interest, and overseas revenues, the home-front result of the league's glitz addiction, as Jefferson noted, was a growing stridency, more ammunition for those quick to typecast and tune out.

Yet, from what I could tell, criticism was cutting across racial lines, from white and African-American sports columnists and fans alike. Following the Puerto Rico defeat, my office suggested a column that would gauge local fan reaction to the latest U.S. basketball degradation. A couple of miles from my home, at the Montclair YMCA, shock was the aftereffect of being slaughtered by a United States commonwealth territory with a population roughly half New York City's.

Most of the lunchtime Y players happened to be African-American and much of what they had to say sounded no different than my interviews with Gregg Popovich or the Italian Ettore Messina. They sounded like the stereotype Kenny Smith had talked about: American players were too rich, lazy, or indifferent to represent their country. They couldn't hit an open jump shot if their $50 million contracts depended on it. They were spoiled and ultimately not skilled enough thanks to our system of entitlement. Again, the larger question that Messina couldn't or wouldn't answer in Treviso had to be raised: Who ultimately deserved the blame for creating this situation, whether you believed it was perception or reality? Players were easy targets, the ones who missed the shots and turned the ball over, but who had created and sustained the chaotic universe of exploitation that empowered the young, celebrated their individuality more than their commitment to team, and hustled them along from one level to the next until they were being hustled themselves?

Just as baseball owners deserved scorn for turning a blind eye and bilking the muscle-ball era we now know was filthy with drugs, the NBA and its corporate accomplices must be the first to be held accountable. When Jefferson, who in New Jersey, was a valued component of an offense praised for its egalitarian grace, worked up a head of steam on the subject of misplaced blame, he sounded wise beyond his twenty-four years, like Magic Johnson, except with the cynical edge owed to a newly developed sense of victimization.

"Myself, Tim Duncan, Allen Iverson—we weren't the guys in there making the rules," Jefferson said. "For ten, twelve years, the NBA has been setting things up for individual talent but we're the ones who get criticized for it, for the way we play. What it comes down to is if we're struggling in the international competition, it's not our fault. People say we don't know how to play basketball, but we're just playing the way we've been taught, the way we've been encouraged to play. David Stern makes the rules. If he tells me to stand over there while someone plays one-on-one, I'm going to stand over there. Of course, there's certain times we all enjoy the dunking, the running, but you know, we look around and we see there is, what, one black owner, and it makes you think about why things are done the way they are, especially when we're the ones getting things thrown at us."

Figuratively, he meant, not in the cup- and coin-hurling capacity that was practiced at The Palace of Auburn Hills (where a fan, not surprisingly, was arrested after hitting Iverson with a coin in an April 2005 playoff game). Jefferson had a clear recognition of who besides the well-paid players was cashing in on the casting of the players as high-wire circus acts and video-game caricatures. He also seemed to be drawing a correlation to what had transpired during the Pistons-Pacers brawl and the predictable and overstated backlash against the perceived unruliness of basketball's young African-American talent base. Jefferson made it clear that he and others believed that they were under siege—and not only from outside the sport—because, in the months following the fight, there were numerous reports of Stern telling NBA insiders that the league was experiencing disconnect from red-state America. As if to validate the reports, Stern hired Matthew Dowd, a Texas-based business strategist who had helped shape George W. Bush's reelection campaign, to create a blueprint for the league on broadening its appeal.

The commissioner was determined to make image-building the central theme of the forthcoming collective bargaining negotiations, pushing harder than ever for a minimum age requirement of twenty to send the message that the NBA was not going to be overrun by what many saw as undereducated ghetto brats. But what Stern called a pragmatic business plan that "affects our business, in terms of our responsibility, the way we are viewed" sounded to me like a hasty acquiescence to the forces of bigotry. The same shortsighted approach took the Pistons out of Detroit and put them in their sterile suburban Palace of Auburn Hills.

To many young players, the strategy was a grander version of the Allen Iverson airbrush incident, an embarrassing episode when the league's in-house magazine digitally removed AI's many tattoos following a cover shoot. Only now, the consequences sounded far more punitive than symbolic, and once again unearthed simmering and racial-related sentiment. Referring to the proposed age requirement, Jermaine O'Neal told an Indianapolis sportswriter, "As a black guy, you kind of think that's the reason why it's coming up."

The quote soon hit the wires and became fodder for the cable and radio talk-show news cycle, an isolated print bite that didn't do justice to the convictions O'Neal had shared in greater detail with me and a couple of other journalists at the All-Star Game two months earlier. He astutely pointed out that if he were old enough to vote, drive, or go fight in Iraq at eighteen, why couldn't he play in the NBA? "High-school players aren't making NBA teams draft them," he said. "You don't want an early entry player on your team? Don't draft him. The reason they are is because these kids are succeeding. I mean, look at the guys who have come in straight from high school." The list of distinguished preps-to-pros players was growing every year, including the rookies of the year in 2003 and 2004 (Stoudemire and James). A 2005 candidate, Dwight Howard, lost out to Emekor Okefor but was widely considered the rookie with the brightest future.

Not surprisingly, the mainstream media wasn't all that enthusiastic about O'Neal's injection of race into the debate, mistaking it for a charge of racism, much in the way Celtics defenders twisted the assertion made by Filip Bondy and myself regarding Red Auerbach. Was Auerbach a racist? Of course not. Did he cash in by pandering to polarized racial attitudes in the marketing of the 1980s Celtics? We thought so and had plenty of old Celtics on the record, in agreement. But, as most public debate on issues political and social increasingly were conducted from extremist positions, O'Neal backed off when he realized that reporters weren't interested in a healthy discussion as much as they wanted to know if he was calling David Stern a hater (he wasn't).

"I think he's talking more about a double standard, a bias," Jefferson said when I asked him about O'Neal. "As young black males, we always seem to be in the position of people telling us what's best for us, as if we can't figure this stuff out for ourselves." Jefferson conceded that "bordering on racism" was probably too strong a charge in either case, but if there was no racial subtext in the treatment of African-American basketball players, he wondered, "Why is it you never hear anyone telling athletes in baseball and hockey that they should go to college?" The question I had been asking in my columns for ten years was finally being raised by the most important people in the sport, the players, at least those who recognized the all-too-familiar strategy in the almighty pursuit of profit: a perhaps paternalistic manipulation of minorities that my old friend Len Elmore, during a short-lived and frustrating fling at representing pro basketball players, described as an old "ACLU thinking that 'we know what's best for you poor, undereducated people.'" Elmore also had a more strident name for those who practiced such subterfuge: puppet masters.

The NBA's expanding global reach notwithstanding, league business fortunes sagged following the Palace brawl and throughout the 2004–05 season, both quantitatively and anecdotally. Regular-season television ratings fell on all three networks broadcasting NBA games, and playoff games suffered precipitous declines on ABC. *The Wall Street Journal* reported in May 2005 that sales in league licensing products sagged by roughly 30 percent. *Bloomberg News* weighed in with a report that claimed many participants in focus groups conducted by the strategist Matthew Dowd said they regarded NBA players as "thugs." During the writing of this book, I found myself having a recurring conversation with many sports fans, some of them sports media people, who told me they hadn't watched the NBA since Jordan retired. Others said it was never the same after Magic and Bird. As a defender of the game, albeit one who had done my share of complaining about the superficiality of the product, I developed the habit of nodding sympathetically but responding, "You're actually missing some pretty good basketball." Because the irony of an NBA season badly blemished by the ugliness of Auburn Hills was that it turned out to be one of the most entertaining in years. The league was a long way from its salad days, but the knockout in Athens and the Palace fight began to look like a potential bottoming-out point.

In several cities, offense returned with a vengeance following the long downward spiral, with overall scoring increasing by roughly 4 points in 2004–05, with as many as six teams averaging more than 100 per game for the first time in five years. In 2003–04, there were nine teams that averaged 90 points or less. In 2004–05, there was one. New defensive rules designed to limit perimeter contact and allow dribblers increased mobility were religiously enforced, but I was just as inclined to attribute the welcome surge to the evolution of the game. More than a quarter of a century earlier, when the NBA merged with the old American Basketball Association, new-era stars like Julius Erving and David Thompson livened up the stodgier establishment. Now, the hard international knocks Americans were taking were forcing them to modulate their style and were making believers out of the most hardened skeptics that the American game needed philosophical change. "Our kids can dunk and make the crowd go wild, but the other countries are playing team ball and at the end of the day, that's going to win," Harry Edwards said.

This was bound to hit home, sooner or later. When the Pistons vanquished the dysfunctional Lakers and the feuding Shaq and Kobe in the 2004 Finals, an important blow was struck for team-first values over me-first vapidity. The championship was a tribute to Larry Brown and, especially, Joe Dumars, the former good guy of the Bad Boys, the Pistons' chief basketball executive who artfully blended the skills of several players as opposed to constructing his team around one or two. "I got more calls from people—many of them not even involved with basketball, just coaches in other sports—saying that our success helped them because we were truly a team," Brown said. "And I think that's what we've gotten away from in our sport the last few years and maybe now we see what the Europeans are doing and we're starting to realize we have to do it differently."

If they didn't, blindness had to be the reason. A growing part of the product, the foreign players—many of whom had tormented the United States in Athens—were, after all, part of the product. In a preseason conversation I had with Nat Irvin, the urban futurist, he foresaw philosophical change in the NBA that was bound to be foreign influenced and stressed that this was something to embrace, nothing to fear. "What will be interesting to watch is how the American game will slowly be redesigned to reflect this new reality," Irvin said. "The NBA will not just be global in name but in style as well." Not lost on him, apparently, was the fact that since the turn of the century, the league's most fluid and high-scoring teams were Sacramento and Dallas, both endowed with major talent from abroad. In 2004–05, the nascent reformation's most significant impact was arguably made by a West Virginian whose NBA career was short-lived and entirely forgettable but who ultimately became a European legend.

I met Mike D'Antoni during the 2002–03 season in Denver, where I was spending a few days shadowing Nikoloz Tskitishvili. D'Antoni had coached the Georgian at Benetton Treviso the previous season, winning the championship of the Italian League, in which D'Antoni had, during the 1980s, become one of the great European pro guards before establishing himself as a successful and decidedly uptempo coach. Back in the States as an assistant coach for the Phoenix Suns, D'Antoni was catching up with Tskitishvili at a sushi restaurant the night before a game and sharing with me his trans-Atlantic views on why the American game had become predictable and stagnant. "A lot of what's happening is because the big men overseas are so skilled," D'Antoni said. "Having big guys who can dribble, pass and step out, and shoot opens up the floor, makes the game much more fun to play and watch." D'Antoni, who had briefly coached a very bad Denver team on an interim basis, promised that if he ever had another NBA team of his own, we would not be watching games that ended 70–68 and were sending the sport back to ancient times, before Danny Biasone had his excellent idea.

Sooner than he'd imagined, D'Antoni got his chance, and at a fortuitous time, when the Suns were unloading expensive, unwanted players and undergoing a much-needed makeover. After replacing Frank Johnson during the 2003–04 season, D'Antoni found himself in his first Phoenix training camp as head coach with a lineup of midsized thoroughbreds and perimeter marksmen and a newly signed conduit, the South African–born and Canadian-raised point guard, Steve Nash. True to his word, D'Antoni unleashed an offense that flowed through the league like a cool desert breeze. Causing matchup nightmares—primarily for anyone trying to guard the undersized center, Amare Stoudemire—the Nash-propelled Suns rang up the most wins during the regular season at 110 points per game, the first time a team had scored that many in ten years. Nash became the first Canadian to win the league's Most Valuable Player award, edging out Shaq, setting off another gratuitous media debate (was the vote slanted to the little white guy?) that reflected a kind of thinking that John Thompson had called "antiquated." Nash had merely been the catalyst for the team that had reversed the most injurious trend in the modern game.

But, while the Suns juiced the regular season and continued their running and gunning ways during the first two rounds of the playoffs, they were exposed somewhat as an aberration, however welcome and even necessary, when they confronted San Antonio in the Western Conference finals. The Spurs had exactly the kind of players Red Holzman was talking about when he pulled me aside all those years ago: They were adept at both ends of the floor, could adapt to any style of play. This Tim Duncan–led mini–United Nations continued to mix athleticism with intelligence, even if the media geniuses and marketing gurus, forever looking for the short cut, the sex appeal, didn't seem to recognize the ambassadorial qualities the Spurs possessed.

If the national audience hadn't warmed to a San Antonio franchise carried since the mid-eighties by the sturdy demeanors of the retired David Robinson and Duncan, it was, in part, because this was the same NBA-cultivated fan base that my friend, Michelle Musler, complained about so bitterly at Madison Square Garden. Many of these fans—along with a good portion of the media—

were brainwashed to measure success on the basis of instant grat-ification and suck-up celebrity. Long forgotten was that Michael Jordan only happened because the league that he and the Bulls began to dominate in the early nineties had established a five-star credibility, thanks to the team-first values of the eighties Celtics and Lakers, of Magic and Bird. Without belief and investment in the core product, without more teams like the Spurs, pro basket-ball had devolved into contrived, overhyped network clatter. Stars drove the hype, but teams steeped in cohesiveness, not com-bustibility, were the engine that powered the sport. Thus real bas-ketball fans had nothing to complain about when Duncan and Ginobili—with a huge assist from Robert Horry—nudged the Spurs past the Pistons to win the third title of the Duncan era, with Gregg Popovich besting his close friend, Larry Brown, in the first championship series in eleven years to go the distance. Fi-nally, a Finals that was more competition between teams than coronation of one leading man or another.

The Spurs and Pistons weren't alone in fostering a renewed commitment to team-based values, and that was the most encour-aging news. The so-called Princeton offense Eddie Jordan helped introduce in Sacramento and New Jersey spread to Washington, D.C., where Jordan, in his second season as head coach, did what Michael Jordan failed to accomplish during his ultimately disillu-sioning two-season comeback in the nation's capital: He steered the Wizards into the playoffs for the first time in eight years. Seattle made itself an elite team with a versatile, aggressive, and offensive-minded team. The Bulls' first playoff season since the Michael Jordan era featured a diverse mix reflecting basketball's new world: a point guard, Kirk Heinrich, who played four years at Kansas and a shooting guard, Ben Gordon, who played three at Connecticut; two big men, Tyson Chandler and Eddy Curry, drafted out of high school; a twenty-five-year-old undrafted Span-ish League import, Andres Nocioni, from Argentina; and a rookie born in the Sudan, Luol Deng, who played one season at Duke.

Tracy McGrady found a stable home in Houston, where

twenty-four-year-old Yao Ming, if not the Chinese coming of Wilt, averaged 18 points, 8 rebounds, and, given his sheer size and technical expertise, was second to only Shaq on the short list of conventional centers. In Miami, where even team president Pat Riley got with the talent-rules program, a slimmed-down Shaq found a much more appreciative young prodigy than Kobe in the refreshingly unpretentious and increasingly unguardable Dwyane Wade. Beyond Kobe, Wade's mind-bending performances in the playoffs drew comparisons with the young Michael Jordan. Three inches smaller and noticeably humbler, Wade was more unselfish, a better passer than the early version of M.J. In the way Kareem Abdul-Jabbar was revitalized in 1979 by the young Magic Johnson, Wade helped Shaq enjoy a resurgent season in which he was celebrated for hoisting a franchise, not pulling down rims.

Understanding this obligation was what turned the supertalented into the true superstar, though many never made the jump, and others had to learn what it took the hard way. Following his disillusioning Olympic experience, a few brushes with the dark side of celebrity, and a slow start to the season for himself and his team, Carmelo Anthony and the Nuggets finished with a flourish under new coach George Karl. Anthony did not make the Denver-based All-Star Game in his own house, the Pepsi Center, as did James, Wade, and Stoudemire, but there was a palpable elation in the air regarding the league's set of sizzling young hands. Kenny Smith called them the most compelling evidence yet that America's inner cities would continue to produce the world's best players "in the way they churn out the most successful rappers because it's part of the culture." Gregg Popovich sensed a crossover appeal, à la Magic and Michael. "I honestly think they are going to be hero-superstars, and it's not about being MTV guys," he said.

Listening to the coaches and league officials sound off during All-Star Weekend from the bandwagon being driven by the newest one-named legend, LeBron, what struck me was how fast basketball time flies, and what hopes the NBA had in leaping from one era to the next. At the interview sessions on the Friday before the game, the young man who carried Michael Jordan's number, 23, on his back, along with the most fervent hopes for an NBA renaissance, nudged his way through a swelling crowd of journalists. "Let me squeeze through, let me squeeze through," James pleaded, before lowering himself into a chair that Kobe Bryant was kind enough to keep warm. Was it a coincidence of interview scheduling or a positional perk of a new pecking order?

As part of a new Jordan Nike advertising blitz released in the days before the All-Star Weekend, Spike Lee flipped through the six-championship storybook that was authored by basketball's erstwhile One and Only, and, in what amounted to a promise that there will be no more comebacks, the commercial concluded by asking, "Who's next?" While it certainly was generous of Team Jordan to acknowledge the possibility of an authentic successor, it seemed that mythmakers inside the league and out had already anointed one. *Sports Illustrated* had just plastered the man occasionally referred to as King on its cover, posing the ridiculous question: "Best Ever?" Not surprisingly, the NBA and its network partners were already trying to wish it so, putting the Cavaliers on television so much there seemed to be a twenty-four-hour LeBron Sports & Entertainment network.

No big deal, James, twenty, called the exposure and fuss. "It's been going on for so long, since I was a sophomore in high school," he said. He added that Jordan hadn't offered advice, nor had he sought out Jordan, on how to deal with the crush of attention, and that was probably a good thing. If James wanted to get a handle on his most important challenge—how not to be manipulated into getting ahead of himself and to pray every night for a better team or a companion star to share the spotlight and the ball—he should have sought an audience with his fellow starter in the Eastern Conference lineup, Vince Carter.

Early during James's second season, the Cavaliers were sold for $375 million to a businessman named Dan Gilbert, an astonishing markup for a franchise that was an NBA eyesore before James, out of Akron, landed so close to home. When James was a senior at Akron's St. Vincent–St. Mary High School, he was practically accused of single-handedly destroying amateur sports when it was revealed that he was driving a Hummer purchased with loans based on future earnings and had accepted free throwback jerseys. When Gilbert, who made his fortune in the mortgage-lending business, was announced as the new Cavs' owner, it was reported that he had been arrested as a nineteen-year-old Michigan State sophomore for running a sports gambling ring. Apparently, African-American athletes weren't the only campus kingpins with bad judgment, nor were they alone in committing the occasional act of basketball sabotage. When Gilbert overreacted to a post All-Star Game slump by firing his coach, Paul Silas, the Cavs crashed and burned and James, despite exceeding all individual expectations, failed to join Stoudemire, Anthony, and Wade in the playoffs.

Edged out for the last spot in the Eastern Conference on the final night of the regular season by Carter and the Nets, James went to the sidelines, along with Kobe and Kevin Garnett, the reigning league MVP, to predictable hand-wringing from inside the league and out, over the loss of such celebrity star power. These people still didn't get it. The obsession with television ratings, and which players or markets were more likely to generate them, typically played right into wild conspiracy theories of biased officiating or outright fixes and ultimately contributed to the perception of the NBA as more three-ring circus than competitive sport. Even Ralph Nader once chimed in, complaining about the officiating in the 2002 Lakers-Kings series. Understandably exasperated by these flights of fantasy, Stern fined Houston coach Jeff Van Gundy $100,000 during the playoffs, for alleging a league-ordered conspiracy against Yao Ming, a claim beyond absurd for anyone familiar with Stern's manifest global-marketing ambition.

What I found more interesting and annoyingly paradoxical about the anxiety over the playoff absence of Bryant, James, and Garnett was that none had ever appeared in a college game. Here they were deemed essential to the league's postseason package, while Stern was lobbying hard to shut the door on high-school players. At least he wasn't trying to snow people that any of this was about higher education, as much as it was about image, about perceptions and resulting stereotypes that impacted the bottom line.

In this case, Billy Hunter didn't agree with Harry Edwards's call on Stern as an "honest broker," in particular for the African-American player. He was more "mindful of the fact that the NBA is perceived as a black product," and on to the way Stern was using his new mantra of wanting "our general managers out of high-school gymnasiums," as a disingenuous negotiating wedge. Upon closer inspection, Stern's campaign sounded more like a code for pandering, as a way to, as Hunter said, "assuage the white fans that think the players are too arrogant, too greedy, too unappreciative." Hunter recognized that forcing American-born players back into the NCAA clutches for at least two years would partially restore the free-marketing system for almost all American-born NBA players. Of even greater significance to the owners' profit margins, delayed entry would impact many players' ability to score more than one long-term, maximum-earning contract, upon expiration of their rookie deals, which were governed by a strict wage scale. As always, it was all about the money.

Some veterans—Grant Hill and Ray Allen among them—supported an age requirement, arguing that protecting at-risk veterans from losing their jobs was an important priority. This was a righteous posture, a good idea, but they were being snookered by the rhetoric of Stern. Preserving veteran's jobs could just as easily be accomplished by giving teams farm-out rights to an upgraded developmental league, providing general managers and coaches the options they needed in distinguishing between an all-world prodigy like James from the work in progress like Nikoloz Tskitishvili, while creating a true teaching vehicle to combat the corrosive adolescent excesses of the American system.

Diversity of experience was something to promote, not legislate against. Tim Duncan had taken the increasingly less-traveled path to the NBA, after four years at Wake Forest. But his team-mate, Tony Parker, had turned professional in France at seven-teen. Vince Carter had come the early entry route, though he returned to North Carolina to get his degree. Yao negotiated his way out of the Chinese Communist bureaucracy, while Dirk Nowitzki had turned pro and played in a German pro league be-fore he was old enough to vote, drive, or go off to war. Many play-ers, not drafted and ignored, went to Europe and Asia and eventually worked their way back. This was the beauty of the league because, in the final analysis, there was no fair way to leg-islate a developmental scale that was growing wider than Yao Ming's wingspan, and that's exactly what Jermaine O'Neal was talking about.

"Let these kids try," he told me. "If they fail, it's because they didn't work hard enough at it. But don't make them go to college to make money for a school instead of themselves, if that's not something they want to do. Don't make them risk getting hurt and lose their one chance at making the kind of money everyone dreams about, if that's not something they want to do." It was a reasoned and impassioned argument and it occurred to me that O'Neal, without a college credit to his name, was making more sense than Stern, the Columbia law grad. O'Neal was speaking from the heart while Stern was preaching out of both sides of his mouth, warning about the evils of high-school players, unwit-tingly endeavoring to overmanage the sport and repeat past mis-takes. In a season when four players with no college credits were in the All-Star starting lineups, when seven made the combined rosters and eleven in all, if you counted foreign players . . . when there were still more than enough upperclassmen left in the col-lege ranks to produce a thrilling NCAA tournament . . . when North Carolina won a national championship with three junior stars . . . when Rick Pitino wound up taking Louisville to the Final Four without any help from Sebastian Telfair . . . who could argue with the premise that American players, though they clearly and detrimentally had too many choices at fourteen, deserved the right at eighteen to decide for themselves?

When Stern's All-Star press conference ended, I followed him and his posse of league officials and security out to the Pepsi Center court, and asked him, privately, how he could rationalize the contradiction of his position, and want to force high-school players into the college meat market he had called (in a conversation we'd had weeks earlier) "so corrupt"? I asked why it didn't make more sense to not trample on the players' rights, just push for farm-out rights to the developmental league and create a system that mimicked the one that had served baseball so well. I mentioned my interview with Myles Brand and his support of a true basketball minor league, the square pegs, the round holes, the inevitable damage to the reputations of young African-American males that ultimately made episodes like the one at Auburn Hills that much worse to live down. Stern listened, nodded occasionally, but ultimately shook his head, refused to see the logic or the light. "Brand says he's for a minor league but his coaches would crucify him," he said. "They want the players."

As if he cared about what college coaches wanted, Stern was now using them as negotiating fodder, even though he happened to be right about their shamelessly self-serving cause. In a telephone conversation two months later, Billy Hunter told me he had received a letter from the National Association of Coaches petitioning him to negotiate a deal that would force players to remain in college for at least three years, as required (and judicially upheld) by the NFL. At least the NFL, while looking out for its own stake in the preservation of the NCAA gravy train and its free developmental system, could make a reasonable argument about the physicality of the sport and the dangers to a body not fully grown. The college basketball coaches' demand was an astounding demonstration of chutzpah, when their business was thriving without the players who left school early or who hadn't gone at all. They were already making out like bandits and yet wanted more control, more pounds of flesh, and more solutions with harsh social implications that were steeped in corporate and self-serving interests.

In the end, the college coaches didn't get the three years they were lobbying Hunter for, but Stern bullied the union into an age requirement, in effect ending the era of preps-to-pros jumpers. Beginning with the 2006 draft, players would have to be nineteen and out of high school for one school year to play in the NBA, though the developmental league lowered its minimum age to eighteen, a loophole for future college-averse LeBrons. Stern also bargained for so-called farm-out rights, allowing teams a two-year window to assign a young player to the developmental league. This was a long-overdue and welcome concession on the part of the union, but one that instantly rendered Stern's nineteen-year-old age requirement unnecessary, nothing more than a trumped-up concession to the colleges in exchange for the promotional benefits of making kids play at least one season under the NCAA big tent. The deal smelled like a sellout of principle by Hunter and his multimillionaire constituents, who were co-opted in the never-ending manipulation by increased cash guarantees. Further, it was announced before game 6 of the Finals, diverting attention from the deserving Spurs and Pistons, another sad and supercilious commentary on the way the game was played outside the lines, from the day the tall and talented flashed their first crossover dribble, from the moment they were tagged and identified as the product. The strings were pulled, the puppeteers went to work, and the players sure learned to dance.

Epilogue

THE 2005 DENVER ALL-STAR WEEKEND at the Pepsi Center was my first since the event was staged in 2001 in Washington, D.C., where the invasion of rich-and-famous twentysomethings from the entertainment industry made me feel decidedly middle-aged, and determined to not return if I could help it. This time was different, though. This time, the gimmickry and glitz seemed more playfully appealing, which I realized had everything to do with the presence of my sons, Alex and Charlie, who were attending their first All-Star Weekend and were perched about fifteen rows up in the lower stands. From my seat in the corner on the baseline, I could see their faces and couldn't help but mimic their smiles as Magic Johnson trotted out for a shooting-skills contest, followed by Diana Taurasi, the women's icon, and all the others, right on through the All-Star Game the following night.

One of the benefits of having sports-loving children, I have come to realize, is being able to view pop culture icons and athletes through their generally, though not always, wider and more innocent eyes. Given the excesses of contemporary entertainment and sports, it can be so tempting to become everyone's grouchy uncle, to disconnect, and drone on and on about more virtuous times, the good old days. As we were walking in the parking lot of the Pepsi Center I felt a smack on the back of the head and turned around to look up at the smiling face of a player I had covered as a young Knicks beat reporter. I called out to the boys to come say hello to Earl Monroe, come shake the hand of Earl the Pearl, once a god on the streets of New York, when a pro basketball game was the classiest show in town, and the Knicks' selfless style of play represented the best that sports could be.

Though they would not have identified the face on their own, Alex and Charlie certainly knew the name, and that Monroe was an integral part of the last Knicks championship team, in 1973. They understood he was an all-time great, and Charlie even took the opportunity to have a second autograph addressed to his YMCA travel basketball team. I could see that Monroe was not only happy to oblige but appreciative of the recognition as the crush of bodies passed without a second look. I, too, had to admit that the exchange between Monroe and my sons, this linkage of generations, put me in the best of moods. Before I began my itinerant life lugging around a computer and a suitcase, Monroe was one of my favorites in high school and college.

Were we better off as pre-cable kids with our newspaper sports pages and handful of television channels? There was no Internet back then, no ESPN, no twenty-four-hour smorgasbord of sports talk and deafening static that occasionally makes me feel as if my head is going to explode. There is so much sensory overload now that I am amazed by how kids are able to process the information, the commentary, the imagery, and come to any clear-headed conclusions about the big, intrusive business of sports. All I ask of my children is that they respect what elite athletes do, understand the commitment it takes, and not engage in cultural and racial typecasting.

This wasn't always easy, given some of the behavior they had been exposed to through the years that was objectionable or worse. For Alex's fifteenth birthday in November 2004, I took him, his brother, and a friend to the preseason NIT semifinals at Madison Square Garden the night before Thanksgiving. Behind us sat a battalion of young men with buzz cuts and scruffy facial hair, who, from the moment they sat down, were jumping up to refuel at the nearby beer tap. With alcohol as their truth serum, they began to get ugly and loud, calling the players morons, monkeys, criminals, and thugs. Just five days after the Malice at the Palace, with security nowhere to be found, the fans in our section were understandably reluctant to complain. The boys occasionally pretended to be amused, though I could see by the uneasiness of their smiles that they, too (thank goodness), were not. As I waited, in vain, for the louts to leave or just pass out, one sardonic thought crossed my mind and I even found myself mumbling it out loud: Where was Ron Artest when we needed him most?

This was certainly no endorsement of what Artest had done, as much as it was my exasperation over what we had to put up with, how repellent these fans were, how much of a tinderbox it was when such primitive attitudes mixed with basketball and booze. And yet, even after what had transpired in Auburn Hills, knowing what it knew about its shrinking fan base, the NBA still seemed more concerned with how image affected the bottom line than with having an honest dialogue about what Billy Hunter called "the elephant in the room." In Denver, the airbrushing of the cultural and racial divide between players and fans became apparent to me when I bumped into Chris Broussard of *ESPN The Magazine* following the slam-dunk contest, while dozens of kids, including my own, rushed the gates near the runway to the locker rooms in the hunt for autographs. Broussard, newly hired by ESPN after writing basketball for the *Times*, had just authored a cover story on hip-hop and the NBA, which he said a nervous NBA headquarters had asked to review before publication. This was a request, he said, that was denied.

Broussard, an African-American, said the story was not a critical piece, merely an attempt to obviate the myths and misconceptions fostered by fear. He and I agreed that castigating the NBA or even labeling it a hip-hop league had become something of a cliché. What it meant, I'm not sure even the critics really knew. Was it based on the mainstream rap blasting through league are-

nas (that was management's decision, not the players)? Was it because many stars typically surrounded themselves with posses of
friends and assorted sycophants (on HBO, the Hollywood version
is *Entourage;* in the White House it is called the president's cabi-
net). What was it, exactly, that critics wished Stern to have digitally removed from the NBA culture?

Allen Iverson was nicknamed The Answer, but his tumultuous
NBA career raised other intriguing questions. In an effective basketball shoe commercial released for the '05 playoffs, shot in a
pool-hall-in-the-'hood setting, Iverson somberly declared, "I'm
not a gangster, I'm not a thug, I am what I am." Over the years, I'd
taken my shots at Iverson, particularly when he fancied himself a
rapper and cut a CD in 2000 that included lyrics Stern called "repugnant and antisocial," and ordered stricken before release
under the threat of punishment. But, as a journalist, I also asked
how Iverson's crimes against morality and good taste measured up
against those of his corporate underwriters. As one who also grew
up in the projects with feelings of isolation from the world outside
the cluster of insulated poverty, having experienced a powerful internal conflict of wanting to change, but not to the point where I
can't remember where I'm from, I have to admit that Iverson's un-
compromising devotion to his roots has often struck me as ad-
mirable, even as he made a decent payday off the persona.

Bearing down on his thirtieth birthday, Iverson was enjoying
one of his best seasons, qualitatively and behaviorally, and during
the All-Star Weekend he seemed to be speaking with sincerity
about wanting to be all grown up, to set a good example for his
kids, and embrace the inevitable role of elder NBA statesman. If
he wished to do so in a wide-brimmed baseball cap, do-rag, and
baggy jeans, whom was he harming? Where are we when freedom
of expression, youthful or cultural, is considered dangerous,
threatening, anathema to an apple-pie perception of what passes
for pure? What would be the extension of airbrushing Iverson and
everyone like him to appease basketball's family-values cru-
saders? Demanding a movement to make NBA imports assume
more all-American names?

While Broussard and I were solving the basketball world's problems, some very un-hip-hop-looking All-Stars happened by: Grant Hill. Ray Allen. Tim Duncan. Dwyane Wade (whose confident yet calm on-court demeanor was being hailed as a refreshing throwback, and who had somehow managed to not be corrupted by the misogynistic, homophobic lyrics of his favorite rap act, 50 Cent). Next, the retired Admiral, David Robinson, stopped by to chat about his faith-based school that I'd visited and written about in San Antonio. Over by the stands, I could see that Alex and Charlie were cleaning up in the autograph derby, landing Hill, Dwight Howard, Jermaine O'Neal, and even the rapper, Nelly, who was featured in full bling on the ESPN magazine cover containing Broussard's story.

Alex later informed me that Nelly was cool, more pop than gangsta, which I figured, albeit largely from a position of ignorance, might be a subject worth its own cover story. For better or worse, that was Alex's opinion and the best I could do as his parent was to help put him in the educated position of figuring these things out for himself. As I watched my boys mix with the other kids, banter with and beg the players, I wasn't thinking about the small fortune I'd paid for the airfare and tickets. I was just happy to have given them an opportunity to come out and take a closer look, make their own judgments, just months after the fallout from the Pacers-Pistons fight. Better they should formulate their opinions on Jermaine O'Neal by looking him in the eye, by the briefest of encounters, than from a mass media drunk on clichés, or an inebriated and foulmouthed mob in the stands. Better, too, for me to keep my middle-aged mind open to the belief that just because the good old days of Magic and Bird were long gone, that didn't mean they couldn't happen again.

As I was saying a whole book ago, lifelong basketball memories could be made anywhere there was a ball, a basket, and the ability to stretch the imagination. My favorite moment of the 2004–05 season did not occur in a playoff game or even a regular-season game, but in the Denver slam-dunk contest, when MVP-to-be Steve Nash continued a season-long pattern of enhancing

Amare Stoudemire's explosive aerial skills in the most superfluous basketball event of all. Angling from the right side of the basket, Stoudemire underhanded the ball off glass, to the other side of the lane, where the shaggy-haired Nash, mixing in the skills of a sport even more globally renowned than hoops, headed it from ten feet out above the cylinder, cueing Stoudemire for the rim-rattling finish. The crowd erupted, more for the setup than the slam, for the brainy demonstration of why pure athleticism was great but teamwork was greater, and why the noggin contained the most rudimentary muscle that quality basketball required. I applauded the trick because it symbolized the best that basketball could be when the stars were properly aligned, when the game was celebrated for power and grace, big and small, black and white. In this judge's view, it was the perfect promotional ten.

Acknowledgments

FOR HELPING CONCEIVE and launch this project before a Palace punch was thrown, I would like to thank Alex Ward of *The New York Times*. Beyond Auburn Hills, I had the great fortune of landing under the tutelage of Martin Beiser and Dominick Anfuso at Free Press, who listened patiently to my diatribe about basketball's ills, then enthusiastically and skillfully embraced the process of turning that rant into a book. Along the way, as usual, my agent, Shari Wenk, helped me weather the storms, those external and internal.

This project could not have been done without the cooperation of my editors at the *Times*: Tom Jolly, Kristin Huckshorn, Jay Schreiber, and Jill Agostino. I would also like to thank past editors, who showed great faith in me when sending me out on the basketball beat: Tom Valledolmo, Jerry Lisker, Greg Gallo, Gene Williams, Chuck Slater, Vic Ziegel, Neil Amdur, and Bill Brink.

Thank you a million times to my friends and basketball-loving colleagues: Michelle Musler, Filip Bondy, Selena Roberts, Howard Blatt, Ailene Voisin, Nathan Gottlieb, Alan Swyer, Liz Robbins, Lloyd Stone, Frank Isola, Paul Needell, Bob Cumins, Sophia Richman, Dave Kaplan, Naomi Kaplan, LynNell Hancock, Arthur Hatzopoulos, Susan Hatzopoulos, Mitch Greene, Ked Novembre, Anthony Colon, and Coach "Earl" Pitts.

Without my family behind me, I know I would never have made it past page one. My love and gratitude go to Sharon Kushner, Harvey Kushner, Randi Waldman, Allan Waldman, Ruth Albert, David Albert, Hilary Albert, Dana Albert, and Ashley Stone. And, of course, to my home team: Beth Albert, Alex Araton, and Charlie Araton. Finally, a special citation is reserved for Marilyn Araton, who despite her best intentions and efforts still managed to raise a basket case. I love you, Mom.

Index

About the Author

HARVEY ARATON joined *The New York Times* as a sports reporter and national basketball columnist in March 1991, and became a "Sports of the Times" columnist in 1994, following eight years as a sports reporter and columnist at the *New York Daily News*. At the *Times*, Mr. Araton has covered numerous NBA Finals, including all six of Michael Jordan's championship seasons with the Chicago Bulls, seven Olympics, seven Wimbledons, and the French Open. His travels for the *Times* have also taken him to Africa and the Republic of Georgia. He has written and reported extensively on the Yankees' World Series prominence since 1996.

Prior to working at the *News*, Mr. Araton was a sports reporter for the *New York Post* from 1977 to 1983, covering the New York Knicks basketball beat. Mr. Araton has also worked at the *Staten Island Advance*, from 1970 to 1977, as a sports reporter, night sports editor, city side reporter, and copyboy.

Mr. Araton is the author or coauthor of three books: *Alive and Kicking: When Soccer Moms Take the Field and Change Their Lives Forever* (Simon & Schuster, 2001), *Money Players: Inside the New NBA* (Pocket Books, 1997), and *The Selling of the Green: The Financial Rise and Moral Decline of the Boston Celtics* (HarperCollins, 1992). His work has also appeared in *The*

New York Times Magazine, GQ, ESPN The Magazine, Sport magazine, *Tennis Magazine,* and *Basketball Weekly.*

Mr. Araton has taught at New York University and was nominated by the *Times* for the Pulitzer Prize in 1994. He was the winner of the Associated Press Sports Editors Award for enterprise reporting in 1992 and for column writing in 1997. Mr. Araton was the winner in the column-writing category for the Women's Sports Foundation journalism awards in 1998.

Born in New York City, he is a graduate of the City University of New York. Mr. Araton lives in Montclair, New Jersey.